The Infinix Note 40 Pro 5G User Guide

A Comprehensive Handbook to Tips and Tricks for an Enhanced User Experience

William C. Wills

© **2024 by William C. Wills.** *All rights reserved.* No part of this publication may be reproduced, distributed, or transmitted in any form or by any means, including photocopying, recording, or other electronic or mechanical methods, without the prior written permission of the publisher, except in the case of brief quotations embodied in critical reviews and certain other noncommercial uses permitted by copyright law.

Contents

Introduction 5
   About the Infinix Note 40 Pro 5G 8

Getting Started 12
   Unboxing Your Infinix Note 40 Pro 5G 12
   Initial Setup and Configuration 15
   Understanding the Interface 18
   Navigating the XOS 14 User Interface 22

Personalization 26
   Customizing Your Home Screen 26
   Setting Up Security Features 29
   Managing Notifications and Do Not Disturb Mode 33

Connectivity 37
   Connecting to Wi-Fi Networks 37
   Setting Up Bluetooth Devices 40
   Managing Mobile Data and 5G Settings 43
   Using Dual SIM Capabilities 46

Communication 49
   Making Calls and Managing Contacts 49
   Sending and Receiving Messages 52
   Setting Up and Using Email 55
   Exploring VoWiFi and Other Calling Features .. 58

Camera and Photography.............................. 61
    Understanding Camera Specifications............... 61
    Tips for Taking Better Photos............................ 64
    Using Pro Mode and Other Camera Features.... 67
    Editing and Sharing Your Photos....................... 70

Apps and Storage... 73
    Downloading and Managing Apps..................... 73
    Clearing App Cache and User Data.................... 76
    Managing Internal and External Storage........... 78
    Backing Up Your Data.. 80

Battery and Power Management................. 84
    Understanding Your Battery Usage................... 84
    Tips to Extend Battery Life................................ 87
    Monitoring and Optimizing Battery Health...... 90

Advanced Features.. 94
    Exploring the Device's Hidden Features............ 94
    Using Gestures and Motion Controls................ 96
    Tips and Tricks for Advanced Users.................. 99
    Customizing User Experience with XOS 14..... 103

Troubleshooting and Support..................... 107
    Common Issues and How to Resolve Them..... 107
    Performing Software Updates and Restores.... 110
    Accessing Customer Support and Repair
    Services... 113
    Warranty and Service Information................... 116

Enhancing Your Experience........................ 120
    Accessories and Peripherals for Your Device... 120

Recommended Apps and Utilities..................... 122
Community and Online Resources..................... 125
Staying Updated with Infinix News and
Releases.. 127

Appendix... **131**
Infinix Note 40 Pro 5G Specifications.............. 131
Glossary of Terms... 134
Frequently Asked Questions (FAQs) for Infinix
Note 40 Pro 5G... 138
Legal and Safety Information...........................141

About the Author **144**

Introduction

Congratulations on getting this Infinix Note 40 Pro 5G user guide! This guide is designed to help you familiarize yourself with your device's features, maximize its capabilities, and enhance your overall user experience. The Infinix Note 40 Pro 5G is a powerful smartphone that combines cutting-edge technology with user-friendly functionality, making it a standout choice for users seeking performance and value.

Unveiling the Infinix Note 40 Pro 5G

The Infinix Note 40 Pro 5G is a testament to the brand's commitment to delivering high-quality devices at an affordable price. Launched globally in March 2024 and set to debut in India in April, the device has garnered attention for its impressive specifications and innovative features. With a 6.78-inch full-HD+ curved AMOLED display that refreshes at 120Hz, the Infinix Note 40 Pro 5G offers a vibrant and smooth visual experience. At its core, the MediaTek Dimensity 7020 SoC ensures that the device can easily handle a range of tasks, from everyday usage to more demanding applications.

Camera Capabilities

Photography enthusiasts will appreciate the triple camera setup, led by a 108-megapixel main sensor that promises detailed and sharp images. The camera system is equipped with optical image stabilization (OIS) and 3x zoom capabilities, enhancing the quality of photos and videos. A 32-megapixel front camera makes your selfies and video calls crystal clear.

Camera	
Rear camera	108-megapixel + 2-megapixel + 2-megapixel
No. of Rear Cameras	3
Front camera	32-megapixel
No. of Front Cameras	1

Battery and Charging

The Infinix Note 40 Pro 5G is designed to keep up with your busy lifestyle, thanks to its large 5,000mAh battery. The device supports 45W wired charging and 20W wireless MagCharge, ensuring you can quickly power up and stay connected. The Pro+ variant stands out with its 100W wired charging capability, powered by Infinix's proprietary Cheetah X1 chip.

Connectivity and Performance

With 5G connectivity, the Infinix Note 40 Pro 5G is future-proofed for the next generation of mobile networks, offering faster download and upload speeds. The device runs on the latest Android 14-based XOS 14 OS, providing a seamless and customizable user interface.

Connectivity	
Wi-Fi	Yes
Wi-Fi standards supported	802.11 a/b/g/n/ac
GPS	Yes
Bluetooth	Yes
NFC	Yes
USB Type-C	Yes

Design and Build

The Infinix Note 40 Pro 5G boasts a sleek design with a premium feel. It is available in various colors, including Obsidian Black and Vintage Green, and features an IP53 rating for dust and water protection. The in-display fingerprint sensor adds a layer of security while maintaining the device's aesthetic appeal.

Your Guide to Mastery

This handbook will serve as your comprehensive guide to exploring all your Infinix Note 40 Pro 5G features and functionalities. From setting up your device for the first time to discovering hidden features and optimizing performance, we've got you covered. Each chapter in this guide is meticulously crafted to provide step-by-step instructions, tips, and tricks to ensure you get the most out of your Infinix Note 40 Pro 5G.

About the Infinix Note 40 Pro 5G

The Infinix Note 40 Pro 5G is a smartphone that encapsulates modern mobile technology within a sleek and user-friendly design. This section provides an overview of the device's key features, specifications, and design elements contributing to its appeal in the competitive smartphone market.

Design and Display
The Infinix Note 40 Pro 5G boasts a 6.78-inch AMOLED display with 1080 x 2436 pixels of resolution, delivering vibrant colors and deep blacks

for an immersive viewing experience. The screen's 120Hz refresh rate ensures smooth scrolling and responsive touch interactions, while the 360Hz touch sampling rate enhances the gaming experience. Corning Gorilla Glass protects the display and features a punch-hole design for the front camera, contributing to its modern aesthetic. The device is available in colors such as Titan Gold and Vintage Green, and it has an IP53 rating for dust and water resistance.

Performance

Under the hood, the Infinix Note 40 Pro 5G is powered by the MediaTek Dimensity 7020 chipset, which is paired with 8GB of RAM and an additional 8GB of virtual RAM for efficient multitasking. The internal storage is a generous 256GB, which can be expanded to 1TB via a dedicated memory card slot. The device runs on Android 14 with the XOS 14 custom skin, offering a range of features and customization options.

Camera Capabilities

Photography is a strong suit for the Infinix Note 40 Pro 5G, featuring a triple rear camera setup with a 108-megapixel primary sensor, complemented by a 2-megapixel macro lens and a 2-megapixel depth sensor. The camera system can record 2K QHD video at 30 fps and includes features such as AI Cam, Super Night mode, and Dual Video. The front-facing 32-megapixel camera ensures high-quality selfies and video calls.

Battery and Charging

The device has a 5000mAh battery, which supports 45W fast charging and allows for rapid power-ups. Additionally, the Note 40 Pro 5G offers 20W wireless MagCharge support, providing users with the convenience of wireless charging.

Connectivity and Additional Features

The Infinix Note 40 Pro 5G supports various connectivity options, including 5G, VoLTE, Wi-Fi, NFC, and an IR blaster. It also features an in-display fingerprint sensor and face unlock for security. The device is equipped with dual speakers tuned by JBL, ensuring high-quality audio output.

The Infinix Note 40 Pro 5G is a well-rounded smartphone that offers high-end features and performance at a competitive price point. Its impressive display, powerful camera system, and robust battery life make it a compelling choice for consumers looking for a device that can handle everyday tasks and more demanding applications. With its upcoming launch in India and other markets, the Infinix Note 40 Pro 5G is poised to impact the mid-range smartphone segment significantly.

Getting Started

Unboxing Your Infinix Note 40 Pro 5G

Congratulations on acquiring the Infinix Note 40 Pro 5G, a device that stands out for its impressive features and capabilities. The unboxing experience is the first step towards exploring what your new smartphone has to offer. Let's look at what you can expect inside the box and some initial steps to get you started.

Inside the Box

Upon opening the Infinix Note 40 Pro 5G box, you will be greeted with the following items:

1. **The Infinix Note 40 Pro 5G Device:** Your new smartphone is the star of the show, and it comes with a pre-applied screen protector for immediate protection against scratches and scuffs.
2. **Charging Brick:** Depending on the variant, you will find a fast-charging brick capable of

delivering up to 45W of power for rapid charging. The Pro Plus variant includes a 100W charging brick, offering even faster charging capabilities.

3. **USB Type-C Cable:** A durable cable for charging your device and data transfer.
4. **Headphones:** A rare inclusion in today's smartphone packages, the Infinix Note 40 Pro 5G comes with headphones, allowing you to enjoy music or take calls right out of the box.
5. **Protective Case:** A custom-fit case is provided to protect your device from drops and scratches. The Pro Plus variant features a case with a MagSafe-compatible connector on the back, enabling the attachment of various accessories.
6. **SIM Ejector Tool:** A handy tool for accessing the SIM card tray, allowing you to insert your SIM card and get connected.

Quick Start Guide and Warranty Card: This is an essential read to help you get started with your device and understand the warranty terms.

Getting Started
- **Inspect Your Device:** Before powering on, take a moment to inspect your device for any visible damage or defects. Ensure the screen protector and case fit correctly.
- **Insert SIM Card:** To open the SIM card tray, use the SIM ejector tool. Carefully place your SIM card into the tray and reinsert it into the device.
- **Power On:** Press and hold the power button until the Infinix logo appears on the screen. The initial boot may take a few moments.
- **Initial Setup:** Follow the on-screen instructions to select your language, connect to Wi-Fi, sign in to your Google account, and configure your security settings, such as fingerprint recognition or face unlock.
- **Charge Your Device:** While the Infinix Note 40 Pro 5G comes partially charged, it's a good practice to fully charge your device before the first use. Connect the USB Type-C cable to your device and the charging brick, then plug it into a power outlet.
- **Explore Your Device:** Once the initial setup is complete, take some time to explore the features and settings of your new Infinix

Note 40 Pro 5G. Customize your home screen, download apps, and familiarize yourself with the camera and other features.

Unboxing your Infinix Note 40 Pro 5G is just the beginning with this powerful device. You'll be well on your way to enjoying your smartphone's benefits and features if you follow these steps.

Initial Setup and Configuration

After unboxing your Infinix Note 40 Pro 5G and admiring its sleek design, the next step is to power it on and go through the initial setup and configuration process. This process is crucial, as it personalizes the device to your preferences and ensures all features function optimally. Here's a step-by-step guide to help you through the initial setup and configuration of your Infinix Note 40 Pro 5G.

Power On and Language Selection

- **Power On:** Press and hold the power button on the device's side until the Infinix logo appears on the screen.
- **Select Language:** The first screen you'll encounter allows you to select your preferred

language. Scroll through the list and tap on your choice to proceed.

Connect to Wi-Fi

- **Wi-Fi Setup:** It's recommended to connect your device to a Wi-Fi network during the initial setup. This allows for software updates and account synchronization. Tap on the Wi-Fi network you wish to join, enter the password, and select "Connect." You can skip this step and use mobile data if you're away from a Wi-Fi network.

Insert SIM Card

- If you still need to, insert your SIM card using the provided SIM ejector tool. The device supports dual SIM functionality, so you can add another SIM card if needed.

Google Account

- **Sign In or Create a Google Account:** To access Google services like the Play Store, Gmail, and more, you'll need a Google account. If you already have one, enter your email or phone number and password. You can create a new account directly from this screen if you still need to.

Data Import
- **Import Data:** You can transfer data from an old device. This can include contacts, messages, apps, and more. You can choose to do this now or skip and do it later.

Security Setup
- **Security:** Set up a security method to protect your device. You can choose from PIN, password, pattern, fingerprint, or face recognition options. The Infinix Note 40 Pro 5G features an in-display fingerprint sensor and face unlock for added security.

Additional Settings
- **Customize Settings:** You'll be prompted to adjust additional settings, such as accepting terms of service, turning location services on or off, and setting up Google Assistant.
- **Software Update:** If there's a software update available, your device may prompt you to download and install it. It's best to complete this step to ensure your device has the latest features and security patches.

Finalize Setup
- **Finish:** After completing the above steps, tap "**Finish**" or "**Start**" to complete the initial setup. Your Infinix Note 40 Pro 5G will take you to the home screen, where you can start personalizing your device and exploring its features.

Congratulations! You've completed the initial setup and configuration of your Infinix Note 40 Pro 5G. Now, you're ready to explore the device's capabilities, download apps, and customize it to suit your needs. Enjoy the seamless performance and innovative features of your new smartphone.

Understanding the Interface

The Infinix Note 40 Pro 5G runs on Android 14 and is enhanced by Infinix's custom user interface, XOS. This combination provides a user-friendly experience with additional features and customization options unique to Infinix devices. Understanding the interface of your new smartphone is key to making the most of its capabilities. Here's how you can navigate the interface and familiarize yourself with its various elements.

Home Screen
- **Wallpaper and Widgets:** The home screen is the first thing you see after unlocking your device. You can personalize it with wallpapers and widgets that provide quick access to weather, calendar events, and more information.
- **App Icons:** Your most frequently used apps are displayed on the home screen for easy access. You can organize these icons into folders by dragging them onto one another.
- **Navigation Bar:** At the bottom of the screen, you'll find the navigation bar, which typically includes the Back, Home, and Recent Apps buttons. These allow you to navigate through the device's interface efficiently.

Notification Panel
- **Quick Settings:** Swipe down from the top of the screen to access the notification panel. Here, you'll find quick settings toggles for Wi-Fi, Bluetooth, flashlight, and more. You can customize which settings appear here.
- **Notifications:** This area also displays your recent notifications. You can expand them for

more details or swipe them away to dismiss them.

App Drawer

- **Accessing Apps:** All your installed apps are located in the drawer. You can access it by swiping up from the bottom of the home screen. Here, apps are typically listed alphabetically, but you can also use the search feature to find an app quickly.

Settings Menu

- **Customization and Preferences:** The settings menu comprehensively lists your device's customizable options. You can adjust network settings, display preferences, sound and vibration, and more.

- **Device Information:** In the settings menu, you can also find detailed information about your device, check for software updates, and access additional features like digital well-being and parental controls.

Camera Interface

- **Camera Modes:** The camera app on the Infinix Note 40 Pro 5G offers various modes such as photo, video, portrait, and more. You

can switch between these modes by swiping left or right on the screen.
- **Settings and Features:** Within the camera interface, you'll find settings for resolution, aspect ratio, and additional features like AI Cam and Super Night mode. These can enhance your photography experience.

XOS 14 Features
- **Customization:** XOS 14 provides a range of customization options, allowing you to change the theme, font style, and the overall look of the user interface to match your style.
- **Smart Gestures:** XOS 14 includes smart gestures that can be used to perform actions quickly, such as taking a screenshot with a three-finger swipe or launching apps with custom gestures.

Tips for Navigating the Interface
- **Explore Gradually:** Take your time to explore each section of the interface. Familiarize yourself with the settings and features at your own pace.
- **Customize Your Experience:** Adjust the settings to suit your preferences. This can

include changing the size of app icons, the layout of the home screen, and the quick settings toggles you use most often.
- **Use Built-in Help:** If you need clarification on a feature, use the built-in help feature or the search function in the settings menu to find guidance on how to use it.

By understanding the Infinix Note 40 Pro 5 interface, you'll be able to confidently navigate your device and take full advantage of its extensive features and capabilities. The XOS 14 interface is designed to be intuitive and user-friendly, ensuring a smooth and enjoyable experience for all users.

Navigating the XOS 14 User Interface

The XOS 14 user interface on the Infinix Note 40 Pro 5G is designed to provide a seamless and intuitive user experience, focusing on customization, efficiency, and security. Here's a guide to help you navigate the XOS 14 interface and make the most of its features.

Home Screen Customization
- **Lock Screen Customization:** XOS 14 allows you to personalize the lock screen with

different styles for the clock, photos, and colors. You can also customize the style of notifications and shortcuts on the lock screen.
- **Themes and Icons:** Dive into the themes section to explore new icons and themes, especially the default theme installed by Infinix. This gives your device a fresh look and feel.

Enhanced Security and Privacy
- **Security and Privacy:** With Android 14's focus on security and privacy, XOS 14 has dedicated features to protect your data. In the settings menu, you'll find options related to security and privacy, ensuring your device and information are safe.

Always-On Display and Animations
- **Always-On Display:** XOS 14 introduces new elements to the always-on display, including weather updates and footsteps. These elements add more functionality and customization options to your device's always-on display.
- **Fingerprint Animations:** Enjoy new animations for the fingerprint unlock feature,

adding a touch of personalization every time you access your device.

Control Center and Quick Settings

- **Revamped Control Center:** The control center in XOS 14 has been significantly revamped, drawing inspiration from the intuitive and user-friendly design of the iPhone's control center. This includes a new brightness, volume, Wi-Fi, and Bluetooth toggle layout.

Smart Suggestions and Quick Start Gestures

- **Smart Suggestions:** XOS 14 offers smart suggestions for your favorite apps based on your usage habits. These apps are transformed into widgets on the home screen, allowing one-touch access.
- **Quick Start Gestures:** Customize quick launch gestures for your favorite apps. By drawing designated letters on the off-screen, you can quickly open apps without navigating through menus.

Enhanced Multitasking

- **Split Screen and Multi-Window:** XOS 14 simplifies multitasking with split-screen and lightning multi-window features. These allow you to run multiple apps simultaneously, improving productivity.

Personalized Entertainment and Gaming
- **AI Gallery and Visha Player:** Edit photos freely with AI Gallery and share content more effectively using Visha Player. These features enhance your entertainment experience on the Infinix Note 40 Pro 5G.
- **XArena:** For gamers, XArena offers a smoother, higher-definition gaming experience with more realistic special effects, ensuring every frame draws you in.

Navigating the XOS 14 user interface on your Infinix Note 40 Pro 5G opens up a world of customization, security, and efficiency possibilities. By exploring and utilizing these features, you can tailor your device to fit your lifestyle and preferences perfectly.

Personalization

Customizing Your Home Screen

The home screen of your Infinix Note 40 Pro 5G is the control center of your user experience, where you can access apps, widgets, and settings quickly. Personalizing your home screen makes your device more enjoyable to use and can improve your efficiency. Here's how to customize your home screen to make it yours.

Changing Wallpapers
- **Setting a New Wallpaper:** To change your wallpaper, press and hold on an empty area of your home screen. Tap on 'Wallpapers' to select from a variety of pre-installed wallpapers or choose an image from your gallery.

Adding and Managing Widgets
- **Adding Widgets:** Widgets are mini-applications that provide quick access to

information or functionality. To add a widget, press and hold on an empty area of your home screen and tap on the 'Widgets' icon. Browse through the list and select the widget you want to add. Press and hold the widget and place it on your home screen.
- **Resizing and Removing Widgets:** You can resize most widgets by tapping and holding them, then dragging the bounding box. To remove a widget, tap and hold it, then drag it to the 'Remove' option at the top of the screen.

Organizing Apps and Folders
- **Rearranging Apps:** To rearrange apps, tap and hold an app icon and drag it to your desired location. You can move apps between home screen pages or to the dock at the bottom of the screen.
- **Creating Folders:** Group similar apps together by dragging one app over another to create a folder. You can name the folder and add more apps by dragging them into the folder.

Customizing Icons and Grid Layout

- **Changing Icon Shapes:** You can change the shape of your app icons for a refreshed look. Access the home screen settings and look for the option to change icon shapes.
- **Adjusting Grid Size:** The grid size determines how many apps can fit on a single page of your home screen. In the home screen settings, you can adjust the grid size to accommodate more or fewer app icons.

Transition Effects and Text Color

- **Transition Effects:** Customize how your home screen pages transition from one to another. Select 'Transition Effects' in the home screen settings and choose from various animations.
- **Changing Text Color:** You can also change the text color under your app icons for better visibility or to match your wallpaper.

Utilizing the Custom Feed

- **Custom Feed:** Some Infinix devices include a custom feed as the leftmost desktop pane. This can be used to organize and categorize your shortcuts or display personalized content.

Game Mode and XArena
- **Game Mode:** For gamers, the Infinix Note 40 Pro 5G includes a Game Mode toggle and settings menu to optimize performance during gameplay. This can be accessed through the system settings.
- **XArena:** XArena is a game launcher that provides various tweaks for gaming, such as notification suppression and an in-game toolbar with convenient shortcuts.

Customizing your home screen ensures that your Infinix Note 40 Pro 5G reflects your style and meets your daily needs. Take advantage of the customization options available through XOS 14 to create a personalized and efficient user interface.

Setting Up Security Features

Security is paramount to your smartphone experience, protecting your personal information and ensuring your device is accessible only to you. The Infinix Note 40 Pro 5G offers a suite of security features that you can set up to safeguard your data.

Here's how to configure these features for enhanced security.

Fingerprint Sensor

The Infinix Note 40 Pro 5G is equipped with a fingerprint sensor integrated into the power button on the side of the device. To set up the fingerprint sensor:

- **Access Security Settings:** Go to '**Settings**' and then navigate to '**Passwords & Security**' or '**Biometrics & Security**,' depending on the device.
- **Fingerprint Management:** Select 'Fingerprint' and follow the prompts to add a new fingerprint.
- **Scan Your Fingerprint:** Place your finger on the power key and lift it after feeling a vibration. Repeat this process until the on-screen instructions indicate that your fingerprint has been successfully recorded.
- **Additional Fingerprint Setup:** You can register multiple fingers for added security. It's advisable to set up the index fingers of both hands for convenience.

Face Unlock

Face recognition technology provides a quick and convenient way to unlock your device using the front-facing camera.

- **Set Up Face Unlock:** In the security settings, look for '**Face Unlock**' or 'Face Recognition.'
- **Enroll Your Face:** Follow the on-screen instructions to capture your facial features. Ensure good lighting and avoid wearing anything that might obscure your face, such as sunglasses or a hat.
- **Adjust Settings:** Once set up, you can adjust settings for face unlock, such as requiring eye-open recognition or improving recognition speed.

App Lock

App Lock allows you to set a password for individual apps, adding an extra layer of security for sensitive information.

- **Enable App Lock:** In the settings menu, find '**App Lock**' or '**Privacy**' and select the apps you want to protect.

- **Set a Password:** Choose a pattern, PIN, or password required to open the locked apps.

Privacy Settings

Infinix is committed to user privacy, and the Note 40 Pro 5G includes features to control your privacy settings.

- **Review Privacy Settings:** Go to '**Settings**' and then '**Privacy**.' Here, you can manage app permissions, control which apps can access your location, and more.
- **Restrict App Permissions:** You can set permissions per app, deciding which apps can access your camera, microphone, contacts, and other data.

Security Updates

Infinix has promised 36 months of security updates for the Note 40 Pro series, ensuring your device remains protected against the latest threats.

- **Check for Updates:** Regularly check for software updates by going to '**Settings**,' then '**System**,' and selecting '**Software Update**.'
- **Install Updates:** When an update is available, follow the prompts to download

and install it, keeping your device's security features up-to-date.

By setting up these security features on your Infinix Note 40 Pro 5G, you can rest assured that your personal information is well-protected. Regularly review and update your security settings to maintain your device's highest level of protection.

Managing Notifications and Do Not Disturb Mode

Notifications keep you informed about what's happening in your apps, but managing them effectively is key to ensuring they don't become a distraction. The Infinix Note 40 Pro 5G offers comprehensive tools for managing notifications and setting up Do Not Disturb (DND) mode to help you maintain focus when needed. Here's how to customize these settings to suit your preferences.

Managing App Notifications

- **Access Notification Settings:** Go to '**Settings**' and tap on '**Apps & Notifications**'. Here, you can see recent notifications or choose to see all from the last seven days.

- **Customize App Notifications:** Tap on an app to customize its notifications. You can turn notifications on or off entirely or adjust specific types of notifications for the app.
- **Notification Categories:** Many apps offer categories for their notifications, such as direct messages, mentions, or updates. You can control these categories individually to receive only the notifications that are important to you.
- **Lock Screen Notifications:** Decide if you want notifications to appear on your lock screen. You can choose to show all notification content, hide sensitive content, or not show notifications at all.

Setting Up Do Not Disturb Mode

Do Not Disturb mode silences all calls, alerts, and notifications except those you allow.

- **Enable Do Not Disturb:** Swipe down from the top of the screen to access the quick settings panel. Tap on the '**Do Not Disturb**' icon to enable it immediately.
- **Customize DND Settings:** For more detailed settings, go to '**Settings**' > '**Sound**'

> **'Do Not Disturb'**. Here, you can set schedules for DND, allow exceptions for certain contacts or apps, and decide if you want to allow alarms or media sounds.

- **Schedules:** You can create custom schedules for DND to automatically turn on during specific times, such as meetings or at night. This ensures you're not disturbed during important moments or while sleeping.
- **Allow Exceptions:** Even in DND mode, you can allow calls and messages from specific contacts. This is useful if you're waiting for an important call or need to be available for emergencies.

Managing Notification Sounds and Vibration
- **Notification Sounds:** In **'Settings'** > **'Sound**,' you can customize the sounds for different apps and system notifications. This helps you recognize the type of notification without looking at your device.
- **Vibration:** You can also adjust vibration settings for notifications. This is particularly useful when you need your phone to be silent but still want to be alerted to notifications.

By taking control of your notification settings and utilizing Do Not Disturb mode, you can minimize distractions and ensure that you only receive important alerts. The Infinix Note 40 Pro 5G allows you to customize these settings to match your lifestyle and preferences, helping you stay focused and productive.

Connectivity

Connecting to Wi-Fi Networks

Staying connected is crucial in today's digital age, and Wi-Fi connectivity is a fundamental feature of the Infinix Note 40 Pro 5G. Connecting to a Wi-Fi network is straightforward, whether at home, work or in a public space. Here's a step-by-step guide to help you connect your Infinix Note 40 Pro 5G to Wi-Fi networks, ensuring you stay online without using your mobile data.

Step 1: Access Wi-Fi Settings

- **Open Settings:** On your Infinix Note 40 Pro 5G, swipe down from the top of the screen to access the notification shade, then tap the gear icon to open the '**Settings**' menu.
- **Select Wi-Fi:** In the '**Settings**' menu, tap on '**Network & Internet**' or directly on 'Wi-Fi' to access Wi-Fi settings.

Step 2: Enable Wi-Fi
- **Turn On Wi-Fi:** If Wi-Fi is not already enabled, toggle the switch at the top of the Wi-Fi settings screen to turn it on. Your device will automatically start scanning for available networks.

Step 3: Connect to a Network
- **Select a Network:** Once the available networks are displayed, scroll through the list and tap on the name of the Wi-Fi network you wish to join.
- **Enter Password:** If the network is secured, you will be prompted to enter the password. Type in the password and tap '**Connect**.' For open networks, tap '**Connect**,' you should be connected without needing a password.

Step 4: Confirm Connection
- **Check Connection Status:** After tapping '**Connect**,' wait a few moments for the connection to be established. Once connected, a Wi-Fi icon appears in the status bar at the top of your screen, indicating a successful connection.

- **Access the Internet:** Open a web browser or any app that requires Internet access to confirm that the Wi-Fi connection is working properly.

Troubleshooting Tips

- **Forget and Reconnect:** If you're having trouble connecting to a Wi-Fi network, try forgetting the network by tapping and holding its name in the Wi-Fi settings, then selecting '**Forget Network.**' Re-enter the password and try connecting again.
- **Restart Your Device:** A simple restart can sometimes resolve connectivity issues. Power off your Infinix Note 40 Pro 5G, wait a few seconds, then turn it back on and try connecting to the Wi-Fi network again.
- **Check Router Settings:** If you cannot connect to a specific Wi-Fi network, ensure the router is working correctly and your device is within range. You may also need to check the router's settings or restart it.

Connecting your Infinix Note 40 Pro 5G to Wi-Fi networks is a simple process that ensures you have access to the internet whenever you're within range of a network. Following these steps allows you to enjoy seamless connectivity and make the most of your device's features without relying on mobile data.

Setting Up Bluetooth Devices

Bluetooth lets you wirelessly connect your Infinix Note 40 Pro 5G to various devices, such as speakers, headphones, and other smartphones. Setting up a Bluetooth connection is a simple process that significantly enhances your device's functionality. Here's how to pair your Infinix Note 40 Pro 5G with Bluetooth devices.

Step 1: Access Bluetooth Settings

- **Open Settings:** Swipe down from the top of the screen to access the notification shade and tap the gear icon to open the '**Settings**' menu.
- **Select Bluetooth:** In the '**Settings**' menu, tap on '**Bluetooth**' to access the Bluetooth settings.

Step 2: Enable Bluetooth

- **Turn On Bluetooth:** If Bluetooth is not enabled, toggle the switch at the top of the

Bluetooth settings screen to turn it on. Your device will automatically start scanning for available Bluetooth devices.

Step 3: Pair a New Device
- **Pair New Device:** Tap on '**Pair new device**' or '**Add new device**' to make your Infinix Note 40 Pro 5G discoverable to other Bluetooth devices.
- **Select the Device:** Once the available devices are displayed, scroll through the list and tap on the Bluetooth device name you wish to pair with.
- **Confirm Pairing:** If prompted, confirm the pairing on both your Infinix Note 40 Pro 5G and the Bluetooth device. You may need to enter a PIN code, which is often "**0000**" or "**1234**" by default, or match a displayed code on both devices.

Step 4: Confirm Connection
- **Check Connection Status:** After tapping '**Pair**,' wait a few moments for the connection to be established. Once connected, you'll see the device listed as 'Connected' in the Bluetooth settings.

- **Test the Connection:** Play some audio or use the connected device to ensure the Bluetooth connection works properly.

Troubleshooting Tips

- **Ensure Visibility:** Make sure the Bluetooth device you are trying to pair with is in pairing mode and visible. Refer to the device's manual for instructions on how to make it discoverable.
- **Restart and Retry:** If you're having trouble connecting, try restarting your Infinix Note 40 Pro 5G and the Bluetooth device, then attempt to pair them again.
- **Check Distance:** Bluetooth devices must be within a certain range, typically around 10 meters without obstructions, to connect successfully.
- **Forget and Re-Pair:** If you've previously paired with the device but are experiencing issues, go to the Bluetooth settings, tap on the gear icon next to the device, and select 'Forget.' Then, try pairing again.

Following these steps, you can easily set up Bluetooth devices with your Infinix Note 40 Pro 5G.

Whether you're connecting to headphones for a personal audio experience or to a speaker for shared listening, Bluetooth connectivity expands the capabilities of your smartphone.

Managing Mobile Data and 5G Settings

In today's connected world, managing your mobile data and optimizing your 5G settings are crucial for ensuring you stay within your data plan limits while enjoying high-speed internet connectivity. The Infinix Note 40 Pro 5G offers various features to help you monitor and control your data usage effectively. Here's how to manage your mobile data and 5G settings on the Infinix Note 40 Pro 5G.

Managing Mobile Data Usage
- **Monitor Data Usage:** To keep track of your data usage, navigate to **'Settings'** > **'Network & internet'** > **'Internet'** and tap on the gear icon next to your carrier's name. Here, you'll see the data used in your current billing cycle.
- **Set Data Warning and Limit:** In the same menu, you can access **'Data warning & limit'** to set a warning level for your data usage. This feature notifies you when you're

nearing your data limit. Additionally, you can set a hard data limit to prevent data usage beyond a certain point, ensuring you don't incur extra charges.

- **Data Saver Mode:** Activating Data Saver mode can help reduce your data usage by preventing apps from using data in the background and limiting data usage for apps running in the foreground. To enable Data Saver mode, go to '**Settings**' > '**Network & internet**' > 'Data Saver' and toggle 'Use Data Saver' on.

Optimizing 5G Settings

- **Enable or Disable 5G:** To manage your 5G settings, navigate to '**Settings**' > '**Network & internet**' > '**Mobile network**.' Here, you can choose your preferred network type. Selecting '**5G/4G/3G/2G**' will allow your device to automatically choose the best available network while selecting '**4G/3G/2G**' can help conserve data if you're nearing your limit or in an area with limited 5G coverage.
- **5G Data Roaming:** If traveling, manage your 5G data roaming settings to avoid

unexpected charges. In the 'Mobile network' settings, you can toggle 'Roaming' on or off depending on your needs and your carrier's roaming policies.

Additional Tips for Data Management
- **App Data Usage:** To see which apps consume the most data, go to **'Settings'** > **'Network & internet'** > **'Internet'** and select **'Non-carrier data usage.'** You can review app data usage and restrict background data for specific apps.
- **Wi-Fi Assist:** Ensure that **'Wi-Fi Assist'** or a similar feature is not enabled, as it can automatically switch to mobile data when Wi-Fi connectivity is poor, increasing data usage.

By effectively managing your mobile data and 5G settings on the Infinix Note 40 Pro 5G, you can enjoy seamless connectivity without worrying about exceeding your data plan. Utilize the built-in tools and features to monitor your usage, control background data, and optimize your 5G settings for the best balance between speed and data consumption.

Using Dual SIM Capabilities

The Infinix Note 40 Pro 5G offers Dual SIM functionality, allowing users to simultaneously utilize two different SIM cards. This feature is handy for managing personal and business lines on a single device, traveling abroad, or optimizing network coverage and data plans. Here's how to make the most out of the Dual SIM capabilities of your Infinix Note 40 Pro 5G.

Inserting SIM Cards

- **Locate the SIM Tray:** The SIM tray is typically located on the side of the device. Use the SIM ejector tool provided in the box to eject the tray.
- **Insert SIM Cards:** Place your SIM cards in the designated slots on the tray. The Infinix Note 40 Pro 5G supports Nano-SIM cards. Ensure they are correctly positioned according to the tray's markings.
- **Reinsert the SIM Tray:** Carefully slide the tray back into the phone, ensuring it's securely in place.

Configuring Dual SIM Settings
- **Access SIM Settings:** Go to '**Settings**' and tap on '**Network & internet**' or directly on '**SIM cards**' to access the Dual SIM settings.
- **Customize SIM Preferences:** You can assign names to each SIM card for easier identification. You can also set your preferred SIM for mobile data, calls, and text messages. If you wish to use 4G or 5G on one SIM and 2G on the other, you can also specify these preferences .
- **Manage Data Usage:** If you're using one SIM for data and the other for calls and texts, you can switch mobile data between SIMs. Be mindful of your data plans to avoid unexpected charges.

Using Dual SIM Features
- **Making Calls and Sending Texts:** You can choose which SIM to use when making a call or sending a text. This can be done directly from the dialer or messaging app by selecting the desired SIM before calling or sending the message.
- **Receiving Calls and Texts:** You can receive calls and texts on both SIMs

simultaneously. If you're on a call using one SIM and receive a call on the other, you can typically hold the first call to answer the second, depending on your network's support for this feature.

Tips for Dual SIM Usage

- **Traveling Abroad:** Use one SIM for your home country and the other for a local SIM in the country you're visiting. This allows you to avoid roaming charges while being reachable on your primary number.
- **Optimizing Coverage and Costs:** If one network offers better coverage in your area and another offers a more cost-effective data plan, you can use two SIMs to optimize coverage and costs.

The Dual SIM functionality of the Infinix Note 40 Pro 5G enhances the device's versatility, making it an excellent choice for users who require the convenience of managing two numbers or optimizing their network usage. Following these steps and tips, you can seamlessly integrate this feature into your daily use, ensuring you get the most out of your Infinix Note 40 Pro 5G.

Communication

Making Calls and Managing Contacts

Effective communication is a cornerstone of any smartphone experience. The Infinix Note 40 Pro 5G provides users with intuitive tools for making calls and managing contacts. Here's a guide to help you navigate these essential functions.

Making Calls

- **Access the Dialer:** Tap the '**Phone**' app to open the dialer. You can manually enter a phone number or select a contact to call.
- **Search for Contacts:** If you want to call someone from your contacts list, tap on '**Contacts**' within the Phone app. Use the search bar at the top to quickly find the person you want to call.
- **Favorite Contacts:** You can add frequently called contacts to your '**Favorites**' for ease of access. This allows you to quickly find and call

these contacts from the 'Favorites' tab in the Phone app.
- **Call Logs:** The '**Recents**' tab in the Phone app displays your call history, including missed, outgoing, and received calls. You can tap on any entry to call that number back or view contact details.

Managing Contacts
- **Access Contacts:** Open the 'Contacts' app to view all the contacts stored on your Infinix Note 40 Pro 5G. You can also access contacts through the Phone app by selecting the '**Contacts**' tab.
- **Add a New Contact:** To add a new contact, tap on the '+' icon, usually found at the bottom right of the screen. Enter the contact's details, such as name, phone number, and email address, and then save.
- **Edit or Delete Contacts:** To edit a contact, tap on the contact to view their details, then select '**Edit**.' You can change their information or add additional details. Select '**Delete**' or 'Remove' to delete a contact from the same menu.

- **Import/Export Contacts:** If you're switching to a new phone or need to back up your contacts, you can import or export them using the options in the Contacts app. You can export contacts to a file or import them from a file or another SIM card.

Dual SIM Management

With Dual SIM capabilities, you can manage calls and contacts for two numbers. In the '**SIM cards**' settings, you can specify by default which SIM to use for calls, texts, and data. You can also assign specific contacts to call from a particular SIM.

Additional Features
- **Blocking Numbers:** If you need to block a number from calling you, you can do so directly from the call log by selecting the number and choosing the 'Block' option.
- **Recycle Bin:** The Infinix Note 40 Pro 5G may offer a recycle bin feature for contacts, allowing you to recover accidentally deleted contacts.

Making calls and managing contacts on the Infinix Note 40 Pro 5G is straightforward. The phone's built-in apps and features provide you with all the necessary tools to keep in touch with friends, family, and colleagues efficiently. Whether you're making a quick call, organizing your contacts, or managing multiple phone lines with Dual SIM, the Infinix Note 40 Pro 5G has you covered.

Sending and Receiving Messages

Text messaging remains a vital communication tool despite the prevalence of instant messaging apps. The Infinix Note 40 Pro 5G provides a seamless experience for sending and receiving SMS and MMS messages. Here's how to manage your messaging needs on the device.

Sending SMS Messages

- **Access the Messaging App:** Tap on the '**Messages**' app icon on your home screen or app drawer to open the messaging interface.
- **Compose a New Message:** To send a new message, tap on the '**Compose**' icon, usually represented by a pencil or '+' symbol.
- Enter Recipient Details: In the '**To**' field, type the recipient's phone number or tap the '+' icon to select a contact from your address book.

- **Type Your Message:** Enter your message in the text field. If you're sending an SMS, be mindful of the character limit, which is typically 160 characters for a single message.
- **Send the Message:** Once you've composed your message, tap the '**Send**' button, usually represented by a paper plane icon.

Receiving SMS Messages

- **Notification of New Messages:** You'll be notified via the notification panel when you receive a new SMS. You can tap on the notification to open the message directly.
- **Read and Reply:** Within the '**Messages**' app, you can read the full message and use the reply field at the bottom to respond.

Sending MMS Messages

- **Attach Multimedia Content:** To send an MMS, follow the same steps as sending an SMS, but tap the '**Attach**' icon to include multimedia content such as pictures, videos, or audio clips.
- **Select the Content:** Choose the file you wish to send from your gallery or file manager and wait for it to attach to the message.

- **Send the MMS:** After attaching the content, tap 'Send' to deliver your MMS message.

Troubleshooting Messaging Issues
- **Check Airtime and Signal:** Ensure you have sufficient airtime to send SMS messages and that your device has a strong network signal.
- **Correct Number Format:** Verify that the recipient's phone number is entered correctly, without any missing or extra digits.
- **Reset SMS Settings:** If you're experiencing issues, reset your SMS settings to default by going to the '**Messages**' app settings and selecting '**Reset to default**'.
- **Clear Message App Cache:** If messages are not sending or receiving correctly, try clearing the cache of the 'Messages' app in the '**Settings**' > '**Apps**' > '**Messages app**' > '**Storage**' > '**CLEAR CACHE**'.
- **Software Updates:** Check for software updates that may include fixes for messaging issues by going to '**Settings**' > '**Software Update**'.

Following these steps, you can effectively manage your SMS and MMS messaging on the Infinix Note 40 Pro 5G. Whether sending a quick text or sharing multimedia content, the device's messaging capabilities ensure you stay connected easily.

Setting Up and Using Email

In today's digital age, accessing your email on your smartphone is essential for staying connected, whether for personal or professional reasons. The Infinix Note 40 Pro 5G, with its user-friendly interface and robust features, makes setting up and using email a breeze. Here's a guide to help you get started with email on your device.

Setting Up Email
- **Access the Email App:** Locate and open the email application on your Infinix Note 40 Pro 5G. Devices with Android 13, XOS 13.5, and likely the Note 40 Pro 5G come with the Gmail app pre-installed, which can manage multiple email accounts from various providers.
- **Add an Email Account:** Upon opening the app for the first time, you may be prompted to add an email account. If not, tap on the menu

icon (three horizontal lines) and select '**Add account**' or find the '**Settings**' gear icon and choose '**Add account**'.

- **Choose Email Provider:** Select your email provider from the list. If you're setting up a Gmail account, select '**Google**'. Choose accordingly for other providers like Yahoo, Outlook, or custom IMAP/POP3 accounts. If your provider isn't listed, select '**Other**' and enter your email settings manually.

- **Enter Your Email Details:** Follow the on-screen instructions to enter your email address and password. You may need to provide additional settings for IMAP/POP3 accounts, such as incoming and outgoing server details.

- **Sync and Customize Settings:** Once your account is added, you can customize sync settings, such as how often your emails are fetched, which types of data to sync (e.g., emails, contacts, calendars), and notification preferences.

Using Email

- **Composing and Sending Emails:** To compose a new email, tap the '**Compose**' button, usually represented by a pencil icon. Enter the recipient's email address, subject, and your message. Attach files or images if needed, then tap '**Send**'.

- **Managing Your Inbox:** Your inbox will display new and unread emails. Tap on an email to read it. You can reply, forward, delete, or archive messages directly from the email view or use the options in your inbox.
- **Organizing Emails:** Use labels or folders to organize your emails. You can create new labels/folders and move emails to them for better organization. This feature is handy for managing large volumes of email.
- **Searching for Emails:** Use the search bar at the app's top to find specific emails. You can search by sender, subject, or keywords within the email content.

Setting up and using email on the Infinix Note 40 Pro 5G is straightforward, thanks to its intuitive interface and compatibility with various email providers. By following these steps, you can ensure that you're always connected and can manage your emails efficiently, whether for work or personal communication.

Exploring VoWiFi and Other Calling Features

Voice over Wi-Fi (VoWiFi) is a feature that allows you to make voice calls using a Wi-Fi network instead of your mobile network. This can be particularly useful in areas with poor cellular reception but a strong Wi-Fi signal. The Infinix Note 40 Pro 5G supports VoWiFi, enabling you to make calls with improved clarity and without using your plan's voice minutes. Here's how to explore VoWiFi and other calling features on your device.

Setting Up VoWiFi (Wi-Fi Calling)

- **Check for Compatibility:** Ensure that your carrier supports VoWiFi and that you have a stable Wi-Fi connection.

- **Enable VoWiFi:** Go to '**Settings**' on your Infinix Note 40 Pro 5G and look for '**Connections**' or '**Network & internet**.' Tap on '**Wi-Fi Calling**' or a similar option to enable the feature.

- **Customize VoWiFi Settings:** You can usually customize settings, such as preferring Wi-Fi for calls when available and managing Wi-Fi calling preferences for roaming.

Other Calling Features
- **Call Recording:** Some regions and carriers allow you to record phone calls. Check your dialer or call settings to see if this feature is available and how to enable it.
- **Conference Calls:** The Infinix Note 40 Pro 5G allows you to make conference calls, merging multiple calls into one. This can be done through the dialer app during an active call.
- **Speed Dial:** Set up speed dial to call your favorite contacts quickly. This can be configured in the '**Contacts**' or 'Phone' app settings.
- **Blocking Numbers:** You can block unwanted numbers directly from the call log or through the call settings menu.
- **Dual SIM Management:** Using two SIM cards, you can manage calling preferences for each SIM, such as which SIM to use for calls by default.

By utilizing VoWiFi and the various calling features available on the Infinix Note 40 Pro 5G, you can enhance your calling experience, ensuring clear communication and convenient access to advanced call management options. Whether you're in an area with poor cellular coverage or want to take advantage of the features your phone has to offer, these tools can significantly improve your ability to stay connected.

Display

Refresh Rate	120 Hz
Resolution Standard	FHD+
Screen size (inches)	6.78
Touchscreen	Yes
Resolution	2436x1080 pixels

Camera and Photography

Understanding Camera Specifications

The Infinix Note 40 Pro and Note 40 Pro+ 5G models boast impressive camera specifications catering to amateur and professional photographers. Understanding these specifications can help users maximize the potential of their device's camera for capturing stunning photos and videos.

Infinix Note 40 Pro Camera Specifications
- **Rear Camera Setup:** The Infinix Note 40 Pro has a triple camera setup on the rear. This includes a 108 MP primary wide-angle camera, a 2 MP macro camera, and a 2 MP depth sensor. The primary camera's large megapixel count allows for capturing highly detailed images. The macro camera is designed for close-up shots, while the depth

sensor aids in creating a bokeh effect for portraits.

- **Front Camera:** For selfies and video calls, the device features a 32 MP wide-angle front camera. This high-resolution sensor ensures sharp and clear selfies.
- **Video Recording:** The device supports video recording in resolutions up to 1440p at 30fps for the rear camera, allowing users to capture high-quality videos.
- **Additional Features:** The camera system includes features such as Dual-LED flash, HDR, and panorama for the rear cameras. These features enhance the photo-taking experience by improving lighting and dynamic range and capturing wide scenes.

Infinix Note 40 Pro+ 5G Camera Specifications

- **Rear Camera Setup:** Similar to the Note 40 Pro, the Note 40 Pro+ 5G also features a triple camera setup. It includes a 108 MP primary wide-angle camera with PDAF and OIS, a 2 MP macro camera, and a 2 MP depth sensor. Including Optical Image Stabilization (OIS) in the primary camera helps reduce blur in photos and videos, especially in low-light conditions or when there's hand movement.

- **Front Camera:** The device sports a 32 MP wide-angle front camera for selfies, matching the Note 40 Pro in terms of resolution.
- **Video Recording:** The Note 40 Pro+ 5G supports video recording at resolutions up to 1440p at 30fps for the rear camera, ensuring high-quality video capture.
- **Additional Features:** The camera system is enhanced with Dual-LED flash, HDR, and panorama capabilities. These features contribute to better lighting, improved dynamic range, and the ability to capture wide scenes.

The Infinix Note 40 Pro and Note 40 Pro+ 5G offer robust camera systems that cater to a wide range of photography needs. From detailed landscapes to vibrant portraits, these devices are equipped to capture moments in stunning clarity. Understanding the capabilities and features of your device's camera can significantly enhance your photography experience.

Tips for Taking Better Photos

With the Infinix Note 40 Pro 5G's impressive camera specifications, including a 108MP primary camera, a 2MP macro camera, and a 32MP front camera, capturing stunning photos has never been easier. Here are some tips to help you take better pictures and fully utilize the capabilities of your device's camera.

Understand Your Camera's Capabilities

- **Explore Camera Modes:** Familiarize yourself with the camera modes available on your Infinix Note 40 Pro 5G. Each mode, such as Portrait, Night, and Macro, is designed for specific scenarios and can significantly enhance the quality of your photos.

- **Use the High-Resolution Mode:** Take advantage of the 108MP primary camera for capturing highly detailed images. This mode is handy for landscape shots where you want to capture as much detail as possible.

Composition and Lighting

- **Follow the Rule of Thirds:** Use the grid feature in your camera app to divide the frame into thirds both horizontally and

vertically. Place your subject at the intersection of these lines to create a more balanced and engaging photo.
- **Seek Natural Light:** Use natural light to illuminate your subject whenever possible. Outdoor photos taken during the golden hour—shortly after sunrise or before sunset—often have a warm, appealing glow.
- **Avoid Backlighting:** Ensure the light source is behind you, not your subject, to avoid backlighting, which can lead to dark, underexposed photos.

Focus and Stability
- **Tap to Focus:** Before taking a photo, tap on the subject on your screen to focus. This ensures that the most important part of your scene is sharp and clear.
- **Keep Your Hands Steady:** Hold your phone with both hands and gently press the shutter button to avoid blurry photos. Use a tripod or rest your phone on a stable surface for even sharper images.

Experiment with Angles and Perspectives
- **Change Your Perspective:** Don't hesitate to experiment with different angles and perspectives. Shooting from a low angle can make your subject appear larger and more imposing, while a high angle can provide a unique overview of the scene.
- **Get Close with Macro:** Use the macro camera to capture the intricate details of small subjects, such as flowers or insects. Getting close to your subject can reveal textures and details that are not visible from a distance.

Post-Processing
- **Edit Your Photos:** Utilize the built-in photo editing tools on your Infinix Note 40 Pro 5G or third-party apps to adjust brightness, contrast, saturation, and more. Editing can enhance your photos and bring out their best qualities.
- **Use Filters Sparingly:** While filters can add a creative touch to your photos, use them sparingly to avoid overpowering the natural beauty of your shots.

By following these tips and exploring the features of your Infinix Note 40 Pro 5 G camera, you can take your photography skills to the next level. Remember, the best way to improve is to practice regularly and experiment with different settings and techniques.

Using Pro Mode and Other Camera Features

The Infinix Note 40 Pro 5G is equipped with a versatile camera system that includes a 108MP primary sensor, complemented by macro and depth sensors, and a 32MP front camera for selfies. Let's explore how to use Pro Mode and other features effectively to help you take full advantage of this powerful camera setup.

Using Pro Mode

Pro Mode, also known as Manual Mode, gives you complete control over the camera settings, allowing you to adjust parameters such as ISO, shutter speed, focus, and white balance to achieve the desired effect in your photos. While specific instructions for accessing Pro Mode on the Infinix Note 40 Pro 5G are not provided in the sources, the general steps to use Pro Mode on similar devices are as follows:

- **Access Camera App:** Open the camera application on your Infinix Note 40 Pro 5G.
- **Select Pro Mode:** Look for the "**More**" option or swipe through the camera modes until you find "**Pro**" or "**Manual**" mode. Select it to enter Pro Mode.
- **Adjust Settings:** In Pro Mode, you'll see various settings such as ISO, shutter speed, white balance, and focus. Tap on each setting to adjust it manually. For example, increasing the ISO for brighter images in low light or adjusting the shutter speed to capture motion blur or freeze fast-moving subjects.
- **Take the Photo:** Once you've adjusted the settings to your liking, tap the shutter button to capture the photo.

Other Camera Features
- **Night Mode:** Utilize Night Mode to improve the quality of photos taken in low-light conditions. This mode optimizes the camera settings to capture more light and reduce noise, resulting in clearer and brighter images.
- **Macro Mode:** The macro sensor lets you take close-up shots of small subjects, such as

flowers or insects, with fine detail. Switch to Macro Mode and get close to your subject to use this feature effectively.

- **Portrait Mode:** Use Portrait Mode to capture beautiful portraits with a blurred background (bokeh effect). This mode uses the depth sensor to separate the subject from the background, creating a professional-looking picture.
- **HDR (High Dynamic Range):** Enable HDR mode to capture photos with balanced exposure in high-contrast scenes. HDR combines multiple shots at different exposures to create a single image with enhanced details in both bright and dark areas.
- **AI Camera:** The AI Camera mode automatically recognizes scenes and subjects and adjusts the camera settings accordingly for optimal results. This is a great feature for quick shots when you don't have time to adjust settings manually.

By exploring and utilizing Pro Mode and other camera features on your Infinix Note 40 Pro 5G, you can enhance your photography skills and capture stunning photos in various scenarios. Experiment with different settings and modes to discover the full potential of your device's camera.

Editing and Sharing Your Photos

After capturing stunning photos with the Infinix Note 40 Pro 5G's 108MP primary camera, 2MP macro sensor, and 32MP front camera, you'll likely want to edit and share these images to showcase their full potential. The device offers built-in tools and features that simplify the photo editing and sharing process. Here's how to make the most of these capabilities.

Editing Photos

- **Access the Gallery:** Open the '**Gallery**' or 'Photos' app on your Infinix Note 40 Pro 5G to view your captured images.
- **Select a Photo to Edit:** Browse through your photos and tap on the one you wish to edit.
- **Use Editing Tools:** Tap on the '**Edit**' icon, usually represented by a pencil. Here, you'll find various editing tools, including filters, crop, rotate, adjust brightness, contrast, saturation, and more.

- **AI Gallery:** The Infinix Note 40 Pro 5G's AI Gallery feature allows for more freeform editing. You can add text, make marks, apply filters, and give full play to your creativity. This feature is handy for personalizing or preparing your photos for social media.
- **Save Your Edits:** Once satisfied with your edits, tap '**Save**' to store the edited photo. You can save it as a new file or overwrite the original photo.

Sharing Photos

- **Select the Photo:** In the Gallery app, select the photo you want to share.
- **Tap the Share Icon:** Look for the 'Share' icon, which is typically represented by three connected dots or a rightward-pointing arrow.
- **Choose Sharing Method:** You'll be presented with various options for sharing your photo, including social media platforms (like Instagram, Facebook, and Twitter), messaging apps (such as WhatsApp and Telegram), or email.
- **Visha Player:** For a more effective way to share content, the Infinix Note 40 Pro 5G

comes with the Visha Player. This feature allows you to freely drag audio files, video files, and documents, making it easier to share multimedia content with others.

- **Direct Sharing:** If you're sharing with another device nearby, you can use direct sharing options like Bluetooth or Wi-Fi Direct. Select the desired device from the list of available devices and follow the prompts to complete the sharing process.

By utilizing the editing and sharing features on your Infinix Note 40 Pro 5G, you can enhance your photos to reflect your vision and easily share them with friends, family, or social media. Whether you're making simple adjustments or creative edits, these tools empower you to bring your photos to life and share your moments with the world.

Apps and Storage

Downloading and Managing Apps

Downloading and managing apps on your Infinix Note 40 Pro 5G is a straightforward process that allows you to customize your device with the tools and entertainment options you need. Here's how to download new apps and manage the ones you already have.

Downloading New Apps
- **Access the Google Play Store:** Tap on the Google Play Store app on your home screen or app drawer. Ensure you're signed in with your Google account.
- **Search for Apps:** Use the search bar at the top of the Play Store to find specific apps or browse categories for new apps to download.
- **Select and Install Apps:** Once you find an app you want, tap on it to view details and reviews. To download, tap the '**Install**'

button. The app will automatically download and install on your device.

Managing Installed Apps

- **Access App Settings:** To manage your apps, go to '**Settings**' and tap on '**Apps**' or '**App Management**'. You'll see a list of installed apps.
- **Uninstall or Disable Apps:** Tap on an app to view its information. From here, you can '**Uninstall**' or '**Disable**' the app if you no longer need it or want to free up space.
- **Update Apps:** Keep your apps up to date for the latest features and security improvements. You can update apps individually or set them to update automatically in the Google Play Store settings.
- **Manage Permissions:** For privacy and security, manage app permissions by selecting an app and tapping on '**Permissions**.' Here, you can control what device features the app can access.

Troubleshooting App Issues
- **Clear Cache and Data:** If an app is not working correctly, try clearing its cache and data. Go to '**Settings**' > '**Apps**,' select the app, and tap on '**Storage**.' Then, tap '**Clear Cache**' and '**Clear Data**'.
- **Fixing Google Play Store Issues:** If you're having trouble with the Google Play Store, such as downloads stuck on pending, try clearing the Play Store's cache and data or check for updates to the app itself.

Storage Management
- **Check Storage Usage:** To see how much storage each app uses, go to '**Settings**' > '**Storage**.' Here, you can view a breakdown of storage usage by category, including apps.
- **Free Up Space:** If you're running low on storage, consider uninstalling apps you don't use, deleting large files, or moving data to an external SD card if your device supports expandable storage.

Following these steps, you can effectively download and manage apps on your Infinix Note 40 Pro 5G, ensuring your device remains organized and performs optimally. Regularly reviewing and updating your apps can enhance your user experience and keep your device secure.

Clearing App Cache and User Data

Clearing app cache and user data can help resolve issues with apps that aren't functioning correctly and free up storage space on your Infinix Note 40 Pro 5G. Here's how to clear the cache and user data for apps on your device.

Clearing App Cache

- **Access Settings:** From your home screen or app drawer, open the '**Settings**' app.
- **Navigate to App Management:** Scroll down and tap on '**App Management**' or '**Apps**' to see a list of all installed applications.
- **Select the App:** Find and tap on the app for which you want to clear the cache.
- **Go to Storage:** Once on the app's info page, tap on '**Storage & cache**' or '**Storage**'.
- **Clear Cache:** Tap on '**Clear Cache**' to remove the cached data for the app. This will not delete any important user data or settings.

Clearing User Data
- **Follow Steps 1-4 Above:** Access the app's storage settings as described in the steps for clearing the cache.
- **Clear User Data:** Tap on '**Clear Storage**,' '**Clear Data**,' or '**Manage Storage**,' depending on available options. This will reset the app to its default state, removing all user data, including login details, preferences, and offline content.
- **Confirm the Action:** You may be prompted to confirm that you want to clear the data. Tap '**OK**' or 'Yes' to proceed.

Considerations Before Clearing User Data
- **Backup Important Information:** Before clearing user data, ensure that you have backed up any important information you might need, as this process cannot be reversed.
- **Understand the Impact:** Clearing user data will log you out of the app, and you may delete any associated files or settings. Only do this if you are experiencing significant issues with the app or want to start fresh.

Regularly clearing the cache can help apps run more smoothly and prevent them from taking up unnecessary space on your device. Clearing user data is a more drastic step that can resolve more persistent issues or prepare an app for removal or reinstallation.

Managing Internal and External Storage

Managing internal and external storage effectively is crucial to ensure your Infinix Note 40 Pro 5G continues to perform well and allows you to keep all your important files and apps organized. Here's how to manage both types of storage on your device.

Managing Internal Storage
- **Check Storage Usage:** To see how much internal storage you have and what is being used, go to '**Settings**' and tap on '**Storage**'. Here, you can view how much storage is used by different data types, such as apps, photos, and videos.
- **Perform Storage Cleanup:** Use the built-in cleanup feature to remove unnecessary files and free up space. This can include cached data, residual files from uninstalled apps, and duplicate media.

- **Uninstall Unused Apps:** Review the apps installed on your device and uninstall any you no longer use to free up space.
- **Move Files to the Cloud:** Consider using cloud services like Google Photos to back up your photos and videos, freeing up a significant amount of space on your device.

Managing External Storage (MicroSD Card)
- **Insert a MicroSD Card:** If your Infinix Note 40 Pro 5G supports expandable storage, insert a microSD card into the dedicated slot to increase your storage capacity.
- **Transfer Files to MicroSD Card:** Move files such as photos, videos, and music to the microSD card. You can do this through the '**Files**' app by selecting the files and choosing 'Move to SD card' or similar options.
- **Set MicroSD Card as Default Storage:** Some devices allow you to set the microSD card as the default storage for new apps and data. Check your device's storage settings to see if this option is available.
- **Format as Internal Storage:** If supported, you can format the microSD card as internal storage, which allows the system to treat it as

part of the internal storage, making app and data management more seamless.

Tips for Storage Management
- **Regularly Review Storage:** Make it a habit to check your storage usage regularly and clean up unnecessary files.
- **Use High-Quality MicroSD Cards:** If using a microSD card, ensure its high quality and speed to maintain good device performance.
- **Backup Important Data:** Always keep backups of important files in the cloud or computer to prevent data loss.

By managing your internal and external storage effectively, you can ensure that your Infinix Note 40 Pro 5G has enough space for all your needs and continues to run smoothly.

Backing Up Your Data

Backing up your data is a critical step to ensure that you keep important information in case of device loss or damage or when performing a factory reset. The Infinix Note 40 Pro 5G offers various methods to back up your data securely. Here's how to back up your data effectively.

Using Google Backup

- **Enable Google Backup:** Navigate to '**Settings**' on your Infinix Note 40 Pro 5G and tap on '**System**' followed by '**Backup**.' Toggle on '**Back up to Google Drive**' to enable the backup of app data, call history, contacts, and settings to your Google account.
- **Choose What to Back Up:** Select the account you want to use for backup if you have multiple Google accounts. You can also choose what data to back up by selecting the appropriate options.
- **Perform the Backup:** Your data will be automatically backed up once you've enabled Google Backup and selected your preferences. You can tap '**Back up now**' to initiate a manual backup.

Local Backup

- **Access Backup and Restore:** Go to '**Settings**' and find '**Backup & reset**' or a similar option. Here, you can access local backup options.

- **Create a Backup:** Select '**Backup**' and choose the data you want to include, such as photos, videos, and documents. You can back up this data to your device's internal storage or an external storage device like a microSD card.
- **Transfer to External Storage:** If you've backed up data to your internal storage, transfer the backup files to an external storage device or a computer for safekeeping.

Third-Party Backup Solutions
- **Use Third-Party Apps:** Various third-party apps on the Google Play Store can help you back up your data. These apps may offer additional features like cloud storage or more granular backup options.
- **Choose a Reliable App:** Look for apps with good reviews and a track record of reliability. Read the app's privacy policy to ensure your data will be handled securely.

Before Performing a Factory Reset
- **Backup All Data:** Before performing a factory reset, ensure that all your data is

backed up, as a reset will erase all data and settings on the device.
- **Verify Backup:** Check that your backup has been completed successfully and that you can access the data from another device or account to ensure that nothing is lost during the reset process.

Regularly backing up your data can protect you against data loss and make it easier to transition to a new device or recover from technical issues. Whether you choose to use Google's built-in backup features, local backups, or third-party apps, the key is to ensure that your data is safe and retrievable when needed.

Battery and Power Management

Understanding Your Battery Usage

Effective battery management ensures your Infinix Note 40 Pro 5G remains powered throughout your day. Understanding how your device consumes a battery can help you optimize its usage and extend its lifespan. Here's how to understand and manage your Infinix Note 40 Pro 5G battery usage.

Monitoring Battery Usage
- **Access Battery Settings:** Navigate to '**Settings**' on your device and tap on '**Battery**' to access battery settings and usage information.
- **View Battery Usage:** In the battery settings, you can view detailed battery usage. This section shows a breakdown of how much battery each app and system process has

consumed over a specific period, typically the last 24 hours or since the last full charge.

- **Identify High-Consumption Apps:** Look for apps that consume a significant amount of battery. Social media apps, games, and other high-performance applications are often the biggest culprits.

Optimizing Battery Performance
- **Adjust Screen Brightness and Timeout:** Reducing screen brightness and setting a shorter screen timeout can significantly reduce battery consumption. The Infinix Note 40 Pro 5G features an AMOLED display, which is more power-efficient, especially when displaying darker colors.
- **Enable Power Saving Modes:** The Infinix Note 40 Pro 5G offers various power-saving modes that can extend your battery life by limiting background data, reducing visual effects, and restricting app activity.
- **Limit Background App Activity:** Some apps continue running and using battery power even when not used. Restrict background activity for apps that don't need to update in real-time.

- **Use Battery Optimization Features:** Take advantage of the device's battery optimization features, such as an adaptive battery, which learns your usage patterns and limits battery for infrequently used apps.

Charging Your Device Efficiently

- **Fast Charging:** The Infinix Note 40 Pro 5G supports 45W wired fast charging and 20W wireless charging, allowing you to quickly recharge your device. Utilize the fast charging feature when you need a quick power boost.
- **Understand Charging Modes:** The device offers various charging modes, including a low-temp mode for charging in cold environments and a smart mode that optimizes charging based on usage patterns.
- **Use Original Chargers:** For the best charging experience and to ensure battery health, use the original charger that came with your device or certified third-party chargers compatible with Infinix fast charging technology.

By understanding your battery usage and implementing these optimization strategies, you can ensure that your Infinix Note 40 Pro 5G stays powered for longer periods, keeping you connected and productive throughout the day.

Tips to Extend Battery Life

Extending the battery life of your Infinix Note 40 Pro 5G is essential to ensure your device can last throughout the day without needing a recharge. Here are some practical tips to help you maximize your battery performance.

Turn On Power Saving Mode
- **Enable Power Saving Mode:** When you anticipate a long day ahead or notice your battery draining faster than usual, switch your phone into power saving mode. This mode limits networking, syncing, and location services and reduces the screen's refresh rate to conserve battery life.

Adjust Screen Settings
- **Reduce Screen Brightness:** Lowering the brightness of your screen can significantly decrease power consumption. Use the auto-brightness feature or manually adjust

the brightness to a comfortable level that uses less power.

- **Shorten Screen Timeout:** Set your screen to turn off more quickly when idle. A shorter timeout can save battery life by deactivating the display sooner.
- **Lower Screen Refresh Rate:** If your phone has a high refresh rate display, consider setting it to a standard 60Hz to save battery, as higher refresh rates consume more power.

Manage Connectivity Features
- **Turn Off Wi-Fi and Bluetooth:** Disable Wi-Fi and Bluetooth when not in use, as these can drain the battery by constantly searching for connections.
- **Disable GPS:** Turn off GPS services when they're not needed to prevent unnecessary battery drain.

Optimize App Usage
- **Close Unused Apps:** Running multiple apps can quickly deplete your battery. Close apps you're not actively using to conserve power.

- **Manage Background App Activity:** Restrict background data for apps that don't need to update in real time. This prevents apps from consuming battery in the background.

Charging Habits
- **Partial Charging:** Avoid charging your phone to 100% or letting it drop to 0% too often. Instead, maintain a healthy charging cycle by charging your phone when it reaches around 30% and unplugging it at around 90%.
- **Unplug When Charged:** Do not leave your phone plugged in once charged, as continuous trickle charging can negatively affect battery stability over time.

Avoid Overheating
- **Keep Your Phone Cool:** Do not charge your phone in hot environments, as overheating can reduce battery efficiency and lifespan. Similarly, avoid using your phone in very cold conditions.

Use Original or Certified Accessories
- **Avoid Counterfeit Chargers:** Use the original charger with your device or certified third-party chargers to ensure proper charging and maintain battery health.

By implementing these tips, you can extend the battery life of your Infinix Note 40 Pro 5G, ensuring that your device remains powered for as long as possible between charges.

Monitoring and Optimizing Battery Health

Maintaining the health of your Infinix Note 40 Pro 5G's battery is crucial for ensuring the device's longevity and optimal performance. Here are strategies for monitoring and optimizing battery health, drawing from the insights provided in the sources.

Monitoring Battery Health
- **Use Built-in Features:** While Android doesn't offer a direct way to check battery health in the settings, some Infinix devices might display battery health as part of the battery information. To access this, navigate to the '**Settings**' app, then to the '**Battery**'

section, and look for any information related to battery health.

- **Dial Code for Battery Information:** Access a hidden diagnostics menu by dialing *#*#4636#*#* on your phone. In the menu that appears, look for 'Battery Information' to see details like charge level, battery temperature, and health. Note that this method might only work on some devices.
- **Third-Party Apps:** Consider using third-party apps like **AccuBattery** for a more comprehensive analysis. These apps can provide detailed insights into your battery's health, usage, and capacity over time. Remember, these apps gather data over time, so immediate results might not be available.

Optimizing Battery Health

- **Adopt Proper Charging Habits:** The Infinix Note 40 Pro 5G series, including the Pro+ 5G model, supports fast charging with the Cheetah X1 chip, optimizing energy consumption and enhancing charging efficiency. To maintain battery health, avoid charging the battery to 100% or letting it drain to 0% too often. Instead, maintain a charging cycle between 20% and 80%.

- **Utilize Advanced Charging Features:** The Infinix Note 40 Pro 5G series offers features like Multi-Speed FastCharge, Bypass Mode, and Reverse Charge Mode. Use these features to manage different power demands efficiently. For example, Bypass Mode can be helpful during gaming or heavy usage, as it allows the device to run directly on power from the charger, reducing battery strain.
- **Manage Power Consumption:** Enable power-saving modes to reduce battery consumption. Adjust screen brightness, set a shorter screen timeout, and limit background app activity. Also, take advantage of the device's ability to monitor current flow and temperature to prevent overheating during charging.
- **Regular Software Updates:** Keep your device updated with the latest software versions. Updates often include battery optimization improvements that can enhance battery health and overall device performance.

- **Avoid Extreme Temperatures:** The Infinix Note 40 Pro 5G series is designed to handle charging in extreme temperatures, including cold charging up to minus 20 degrees Celsius. However, for optimal battery health, avoid exposing your device to extreme hot or cold temperatures for prolonged periods.

By closely monitoring your battery's health and adopting these optimization strategies, you can ensure that your Infinix Note 40 Pro 5G remains powered and performs efficiently over time.

Advanced Features

Exploring the Device's Hidden Features

The Infinix Note 40 Pro 5G, along with its variants in the Hot 40 series, is packed with many hidden features and settings that can enhance your user experience. These features are designed to improve functionality, provide shortcuts, and customize your device to suit your needs better. Let's explore some of these hidden features and how to access them.

Accessing Hidden Features
- **Secret Codes:** The Infinix Hot 40 Pro, for instance, allows users to access hidden menus and information by entering specific codes into the phone dialer. For example, entering *#06# displays the device's IMEI number. While not all codes are publicly shared, they can offer insights into the device's system and functionalities.
- **FCM Diagnostics:** By dialing *#*#426#*#*, users can access FCM

Diagnostics. This feature is handy for developers or users interested in the device's Firebase Cloud Messaging diagnostics.

- **Smart Panel:** The Smart Panel is a customizable sidebar that provides quick access to frequently used apps and tools. It can be accessed by sliding from the edge of the smartphone's screen. This feature is highly convenient for multitasking and quickly switching between apps.

- **App Lock:** For added privacy, the Infinix Hot 40 series includes an App Lock feature that allows users to set a PIN, pattern, or password for individual apps. This ensures that sensitive information within apps is protected from unauthorized access.

- **Eye Care Mode:** The Eye Care option is designed for users who spend much time on their smartphones, whether for work, gaming, or watching movies. It adjusts the screen's color temperature to reduce eye strain, especially during prolonged use. Users can customize the intensity and automatically schedule the Eye Care mode to activate during specific times.

- **Automatic Deletion for WhatsApp:** A specific feature mentioned for WhatsApp allows the automatic deletion of messages based on user-defined settings. This can help manage storage and keep conversations tidy without manual intervention.
- **Customizable Navigation Buttons:** Users can customize the layout and functionality of the navigation buttons according to their preferences. This feature provides a more personalized and efficient navigation experience.

Users can significantly enhance their experience with the Infinix Note 40 Pro 5G and its variants by exploring and utilizing these hidden features. Whether it's improving device security with App Lock, reducing eye strain with Eye Care mode, or accessing frequently used apps quickly with the Smart Panel, these features add a layer of convenience and customization to the device.

Using Gestures and Motion Controls

The Infinix Note 40 Pro 5G, along with other models like the Infinix Hot 40i, incorporates a variety of gestures and motion controls that can enhance the user experience by providing quick and intuitive ways to interact with the device. Here's how to use these features effectively.

Quick Start Gestures
- **Enable Quick Start:** Access '**Settings**,' navigate to '**Special Functions**,' and select '**Actions and Gestures**.' You can enable the '**Quick Start**' function.
- **Customize Gestures:** Within the Quick Start menu, you can assign specific actions to certain gestures. For example, drawing a '**W**' on the locked screen can be set to open the contacts app or any other app of your choice.

Screen Gestures
- **Double Tap to Wake or Lock:** You can double-tap the screen to wake it up or lock it when the device is locked. This feature can be enabled in the 'Actions and Gestures' settings.
- **Music Control Gestures:** Control music playback directly from the lock screen using gestures. Draw a line to the right to play the next track, to the left for the previous track, or draw a pause symbol to play or pause the music.

Motion Controls
- **Flip to Mute:** Activate the '**Flip to Mute**' gesture to easily mute incoming calls by flipping the phone screen down onto a surface.
- **Raise to Ear:** The '**Raise to Ear**' motion allows you to answer calls automatically by simply raising the phone to your ear.
- **Lift to Wake:** With '**Lift to Wake**' enabled, you can pick up your device, and the screen will wake up without pressing any buttons.

Call Gestures
- **Unir Call with a Gesture:** Enable this function to answer calls by placing two fingers in front of the camera or showing the entire palm of your hand to decline a call.

Screenshot Gestures
- **Three-Finger Screenshot:** Swipe down with three fingers on the screen to take a screenshot. You can also hold three fingers on the screen to take a partial screenshot, selecting only the area you want to capture.
- **Scroll Shot:** To capture an entire webpage or document, use the scroll shot by pressing

the power and volume down buttons simultaneously and holding them for a few seconds.

- **Delete Screenshot with Gesture:** After taking a screenshot, you can quickly delete it by dragging it to the bottom of the screen.

By utilizing these gestures and motion controls, you can easily navigate your Infinix Note 40 Pro 5G and perform common tasks. These features are designed to make your interaction with the device faster and more convenient, allowing for a more seamless user experience.

Tips and Tricks for Advanced Users

For advanced Infinix Note 40 Pro 5G users, several tips and tricks can unlock additional functionality and enhance the overall experience with the device. Here are some advanced tips:

Utilizing MagCharge Technology

- **Maximize Charging Efficiency:** Take advantage of the 20W Wireless MagCharge technology for a convenient and fast charging experience. Use the Infinix MagKit, which includes the MagCase, MagPad, and

MagPower, to optimize the charging process and maintain battery health.

Exploring Developer Options

- **Access Developer Options:** To enable Developer Options, go to '**Settings**,' tap on '**About phone**,' and repeatedly tap on '**Build number**' until you see a message that Developer Options have been unlocked. Once enabled, you can hide Developer Options by toggling them off in the 'System' section of the settings.

Recovery Mode

- **Enter Recovery Mode:** To perform advanced actions like factory resets or wiping the cache partition, boot your Infinix Hot 40 Pro into Recovery Mode. This can typically be done by turning off the device and simultaneously holding the power and volume-up buttons until the recovery menu appears.

Advanced Camera Features

- **Leverage In-Sensor Zoom:** Use the 108MP main camera's in-sensor zoom technology to capture distant subjects with 3x

Lossless Superzoom, maintaining image clarity and details. Combine this with Optical Image Stabilization (OIS) for sharper and more stable shots.

Mobile Gaming Enhancements

- **Optimize Gaming Performance:** Utilize the XBOOST Frame Rate Control to optimize performance for popular MOBA and FPS games. The vacuum chamber cooling system can reduce temperatures by up to 7°C, ensuring your device stays cool during intense gaming sessions.

Smart Panel and Gestures

- **Customize the Smart Panel:** Enable and personalize the Smart Panel for quick access to frequently used apps and tools. This feature can be accessed by sliding from the edge of the screen.

Dual Video Mode

- **Record with Front and Rear Cameras:** Use Dual Video mode to simultaneously record from the 32MP front and rear cameras, capturing events from different perspectives.

AI Features
- **Explore AI Capabilities:** Engage with AI features like Folax, Ask AI, and the AI wallpaper generator to enhance creativity and productivity. These features are part of the XOS 14 installed on all models of the NOTE 40 Series.

Sound Quality
- **Experience Enhanced Audio:** Enjoy immersive sound quality with dual stereo speakers fine-tuned by JBL engineers, which can significantly improve your gaming and media consumption experience.

By exploring these advanced features and settings, users can take full advantage of the capabilities of the Infinix Note 40 Pro 5G and other models in the series. Whether it's optimizing the device for gaming, using advanced camera functions, or customizing the user interface, these tips can help advanced users tailor their devices to their specific needs and preferences.

Customizing User Experience with XOS 14

XOS 14, the custom user interface on the Infinix Note 40 Pro 5G, offers a range of features that allow users to personalize their experience and make the most of their device. Here are some tips for customizing the user experience with XOS 14.

Lock Screen Customization
- **Personalize the Lock Screen:** With XOS 14, you can change the style of the clock, photos, and colors on the lock screen. You can also customize the style of notifications and shortcuts, giving you control over the look and functionality of your lock screen.

Always-On Display
- **Add Elements to Always-On Display:** XOS 14 introduces new elements to the always-on display, such as weather updates and footsteps. These elements can be added to the always-on display, providing useful information at a glance.

Control Center and Notifications
- **Revamped Control Center:** The control center in XOS 14 has been redesigned to

resemble the intuitive layout found on the iPhone, with similar brightness, volume, Wi-Fi, and Bluetooth toggles. This provides a familiar and user-friendly experience for accessing quick settings.
- **Magic Ring Notifications:** XOS 14 introduces the Magic Ring, Infinix's version of Apple's Dynamic Island, which offers a new way to interact with notifications and ongoing activities.

Themes and Icons
- **Explore New Themes and Icons:** The update brings new icons and themes, especially the default theme installed by Infinix, which features a near-future style combining virtual and reality. The Theming engine includes an online repository for additional customization options.

Smart Suggestions and Quick Start Gestures
- **Access Favorite Apps with Smart Suggestions:** Based on your usage habits, XOS 14 transforms your favorite apps into widgets on the home screen, allowing

one-touch access and a glance at important information.

- **Use Quick Start Gestures:** Customize quick launch gestures for your favorite apps by drawing designated letters off-screen. This personalizes your phone to quickly open apps without navigating menus.

Gaming Enhancements
- **Optimize Gaming with XBOOST:** For gamers, XBOOST Frame Rate Control optimizes performance for popular MOBA and FPS games. At the same time, the vacuum chamber cooling system reduces temperatures by up to 7°C for a smoother gaming experience.

AI Features
- **Engage with AI Capabilities:** XOS 14 enhances creativity and productivity with AI features like Folax, Ask AI, and the AI wallpaper generator. These features provide a more intelligent and personalized user experience.

Sound Quality

- **Experience Enhanced Audio:** The dual stereo speakers fine-tuned by JBL engineers offer immersive sound quality, which can significantly improve your media consumption and gaming experience.

Users can use these customization options to tailor their Infinix Note 40 Pro 5G to fit their personal style and usage preferences. XOS 14 provides a flexible and feature-rich platform that enhances the overall user experience.

Troubleshooting and Support

Common Issues and How to Resolve Them

Even the most reliable smartphones can encounter issues. For users of the Infinix Note 40 Pro 5G and other models like the Infinix Hot 40 Pro, here are some common problems and their potential solutions.

Not Turning On or Freezing

- **Force Restart:** If your Infinix device is not turning on or freezing, try a force restart by holding the power button for about 10 seconds.
- **Charge the Device:** Ensure the device is charged. Check the charger, cable, and power source if it's not charging. Clean the charging port with a soft, dry cloth to remove debris.

Overheating

- **Close Unnecessary Apps:** Overheating can occur when too many apps are running. Close apps that are not in use to reduce the load on the processor.
- **Avoid Heavy Gaming:** Intense gaming can cause your device to heat up. Take breaks between gaming sessions to allow the device to cool down.
- **Remove the Case:** Removing the phone case can sometimes help dissipate heat more effectively.

Not Charging

- **Check the Charger and Cable:** Use the original charger and cable or certified third-party chargers. Inspect them for any damage.
- **Clean the Charging Port:** Dust and debris in the charging port can prevent proper contact. Clean it carefully with a toothpick or small brush.

Not Connecting (Wi-Fi, Bluetooth)

- **Toggle Connectivity:** Turn off Wi-Fi or Bluetooth and then turn it back on.

Sometimes, a simple toggle can resolve connectivity issues.

- **Restart the Device:** A restart can refresh the system and resolve connectivity problems.
- **Forget Network or Unpair Device:** In Wi-Fi settings, forget the network and reconnect. For Bluetooth, unpair the device and pair it again.

SIM Card Registration Failed

- **Reinsert SIM Card:** Power off the device, remove the SIM card, and reinsert it to ensure it's properly seated in the tray.
- **Check for Carrier Issues:** Contact your carrier to ensure there are no issues with your account or network coverage.

No Internet Service

- **Check Data Settings:** Ensure mobile data is turned on, and you have an active data plan. Check APN settings if necessary.
- **Restart the Device:** Sometimes, a simple restart can restore internet connectivity.

Slow Performance

- **Clear Cache:** Regularly clear the cache of your apps to free up memory and improve performance.

- **Update Software:** Ensure your device runs the latest software version for optimal performance and security.

Security Patch Updates

- **Check for Updates:** If your device is no longer receiving security patches, manually check for any available updates in the 'Settings' under 'System update'.

For more complex issues or if these solutions do not resolve the problem, visiting a service center for professional assistance may be necessary. Always back up your data before attempting any troubleshooting that could lead to data loss.

Performing Software Updates and Restores

Keeping your Infinix Note 40 Pro 5G up to date with the latest software updates is crucial for ensuring optimal performance, security, and access to new features. Additionally, knowing how to restore your device can be invaluable in troubleshooting issues or resetting the device to its original state. Here's how to perform software updates and restores.

Performing Software Updates
- **Check for Updates:** Regularly check for software updates to ensure your device runs the latest version. Navigate to **'Settings'** > **'System'** > **'System updates**.' Here, your device will automatically check for available updates.
- **Download and Install Updates:** If an update is available, you'll see an option to download it. Ensure you're connected to Wi-Fi to avoid using your mobile data. Once downloaded, you can install the update. Your device may restart several times during the installation process.
- **Update Apps:** Remember to keep your apps updated. Open the Google Play Store, tap on your profile icon, and select **'Manage apps & device**.' Here, you can update individual apps or select **'Update all'** to update all apps at once.

Performing a Factory Reset (Restore)

- **Backup Your Data:** Ensure all important data is backed up before performing a factory reset. You can use Google's backup feature, a third-party app, or manually transfer files to a computer or cloud storage.
- **Reset from Settings (Password Required):** If you can access your device, the easiest way to perform a factory reset is through the settings. Navigate to '**Settings**' > '**System**' > '**Reset** options' > '**Erase all data (factory reset)**.' Follow the prompts to complete the reset.
- **Using Recovery Mode:** If you cannot access your device due to a forgotten password or severe software issues, you can use Recovery Mode. Power off your device, then press and hold the '**Volume Up + Power**' buttons simultaneously until the Infinix logo appears. Use the volume buttons to navigate to '**wipe data/factory reset**' and the power button to select it. Confirm the reset; your device will restart as new.
- **After the Reset:** Once the reset is complete, you'll need to set up your device as if it were new. This includes logging into your Google

account, restoring your data, and reinstalling apps.

By regularly updating your Infinix Note 40 Pro 5G and knowing how to restore it when necessary, you can enjoy a smooth, secure, and up-to-date user experience. Remember, a factory reset should be a last resort, as it erases all data on the device.

Accessing Customer Support and Repair Services

For Infinix Note 40 Pro 5G users and other Infinix device owners, accessing customer support and repair services is straightforward, ensuring you can quickly find solutions to any issues you might encounter. Here's a comprehensive guide on how to access these services.

Contacting Infinix Customer Support
- **Phone Support:** You can reach Infinix Mobile Customer Service directly by calling **+861 800 419 0525**. This line provides access to various customer service options, including technical support and inquiries about products or services.

- **Email Support:** For less urgent inquiries or to document your issue in detail, you can email Infinix Mobile's customer service at **hello@infinixmobility.com.** This method is suitable for legal, privacy inquiries, sales/reservations, and technical support.
- **Official Website and Help Center:** Visit Infinix's official website **(https://wap.infinixmobility.com/care/ support)** for product support, to find a repair center, learn about the limited warranty, and access FAQs. The website also offers a platform to connect with other Infinix users or get professional advice from Infinix.

Locating Repair Services
- **Carlcare Service Centers:** Carlcare is the official service center for Infinix, providing professional repair and maintenance services for mobile phones, computers, tablets, and more. Visit the Carlcare website **(https://www.carlcare.com/global/)** to locate an official service center, check spare parts prices, and check the warranty status for your device.

- **Infinix Authorized Repair Services:** Infinix has authorized repair services that can handle various issues, from screen replacements to more complex repairs—visit (https://getitfixed.uk/brands/infinix-brand-page/) for local expert out-of-warranty Infinix repair services nationwide.
- **Infinix Repair and Service Centres:** For users in specific regions like India, you can find your nearest repair center by visiting (https://www.infinixmobiles.in/repair-center/). This page provides information on phone repair services, TV repair services, and business solutions.
- **Online Support and Appointment Booking:** For convenience, you can book an appointment and drop off your device at a repair center using online services. Some service providers offer mail-in services, allowing you to send your device to their repair headquarters.

Additional Support Options
- **Community and Forums:** Engage with the Infinix community through forums and social media platforms. These can be valuable

resources for troubleshooting and tips and advice from other Infinix users.

- **FAQs and Online Manuals:** The Infinix support website and Carlcare offer extensive FAQs and online manuals to help resolve common issues without contacting customer support.

By utilizing these customer support and repair service options, Infinix users can ensure their devices remain in top condition, with access to professional assistance whenever needed.

Warranty and Service Information

For Infinix Note 40 Pro 5G users, understanding the warranty and service information is crucial for ensuring you can access repair and maintenance services when needed. Here's a comprehensive overview of the warranty and service information.

Warranty Coverage
- **Limited Warranty Period:** The Infinix Note 40 Pro 5G comes with a one-year hardware repair coverage limited warranty. This warranty covers defects in materials and workmanship under normal use.

- **What's Covered:** The warranty typically includes the smartphone itself, built-in battery, charger, cable, and headset that come in the box. Retail accessories like data cables, chargers, headsets, mobile power, smartwatches, soundboxes, smart bracelets, and smart life products also come with a 12-month warranty. Home appliances like TVs are covered for 12 months as well.
- **Exclusions:** The warranty does not cover consumable parts like batteries or protective coatings designed to diminish over time unless a failure occurs due to a material or workmanship defect. It also excludes cosmetic damage, damage caused by accident, abuse, liquid contact, fire, earthquake, or external cause, and damage caused by service performed by any unauthorized service provider. Additionally, the warranty does not cover products that have been modified without written permission or defects caused by normal wear and tear or otherwise due to the normal aging of the product.

Service Information

- **Carlcare Service Centers:** For repair and maintenance services, Infinix users can visit Carlcare Service Centers, the official service provider for Infinix. Carlcare provides professional repair services for smartphones, computers, tablets, and more. Users can visit the Carlcare website to locate an official service center, check spare parts prices, and check the warranty status for their device.
- **Contacting Customer Support:** For warranty service, complaints regarding the site, or further information regarding the use of the site, users can contact Infinix customer support using the provided contact details. This includes a phone number, fax number, and email address for TIS International (USA), Inc., doing business as Infinix Healthcare.
- **Online Support and Appointment Booking:** Users can access support, learn about products, view online manuals, get the latest downloads, and more through the Infinix official website. Additionally, users can connect with other Infinix users or get

service, support, and professional advice from Infinix through the website.

By understanding the warranty and service information for the Infinix Note 40 Pro 5G, users can ensure they are well informed about their rights and options for repair and maintenance services.

Enhancing Your Experience

Accessories and Peripherals for Your Device

To further enhance the experience of using the Infinix Note 40 Pro 5G, incorporating accessories and peripherals can significantly add to the device's functionality, protection, and overall enjoyment. Here are some recommended accessories and peripherals for the Infinix Note 40 Pro 5G.

Infinix MagCharge Accessory Kit

The Infinix MagCharge accessory kit is designed to provide a convenient magnetic charging experience. The kit includes:

- **GaN 68W Fast Charger:** Offers efficient and rapid charging for your device.
- **MagCase:** A phone case designed to work with the magnetic charging system, ensuring your phone stays protected while charging.

- **MagPad:** A magnetic charging pad that attaches to the back of your device for a secure charging connection.
- **MagPower:** A magnetic power bank with a 3020mAh built-in battery, offering additional power on the go.

These accessories are specifically designed to enhance the charging experience of your Infinix Note 40 Pro 5G, providing fast, efficient, and convenient charging options.

Audio Peripherals

- **JBL-Branded Audio:** The Infinix Note 40 Pro 5G is recognized for its excellent sound quality, good bass, balanced timbre, and rich detail at high frequencies. It reproduces natural sound quality and can be branded with JBL. Consider adding JBL headphones or speakers to your setup for an enhanced audio experience.

Protective Cases

- **Nillkin Super Frosted Shield Matte Cover Case:** This case offers a sleek, matte finish that provides excellent grip and protection without adding bulk to your device.

It's designed for the Infinix Note 40 Pro series, ensuring a perfect fit.

Additional Peripherals

While specific peripherals like processors, graphic cards, and motherboards mentioned in the sources are not directly applicable to smartphones, investing in compatible peripherals like Bluetooth keyboards, mice, and external storage solutions can further enhance productivity and entertainment experiences with your Infinix Note 40 Pro 5G.

By integrating these accessories and peripherals, you can protect your device, improve its functionality, and enjoy a superior user experience. Whether it's through advanced charging solutions, high-quality audio peripherals, or protective cases, these additions can make your Infinix Note 40 Pro 5G even more versatile and enjoyable to use.

Recommended Apps and Utilities

No specific apps or utilities are directly recommended for the Infinix Note 40 Pro 5G. However, considering the features and capabilities of the Infinix Note 40 Pro 5G as described, here are some recommended apps and utilities that could enhance the user experience of the device:

Productivity Apps
- **Microsoft Office:** For creating and editing documents, spreadsheets, and presentations on the go.
- **Google Keep:** A note-taking app that allows you to quickly capture what's on your mind and get a reminder later at the right place or time.

Photography and Video Editing Apps
- **Adobe Lightroom:** Offers advanced photo editing capabilities to enhance your photos taken with the 108MP primary camera.
- **InShot:** A powerful video editing app that allows you to trim, speed up, and add music and effects to your videos.

Entertainment and Streaming
- **Spotify:** For streaming music and podcasts with the enhanced audio experience provided by JBL-branded audio.
- **Netflix:** Offers a wide range of TV shows, movies, anime, documentaries, and more on thousands of internet-connected devices.

Health and Fitness
- **MyFitnessPal:** Track your diet and exercise in one place to reach your fitness goals.
- **Strava:** Track your runs and cycling sessions to analyze your performance over time.

Utility Apps
- **LastPass:** A password manager that stores encrypted passwords online.
- **Google Drive:** Cloud storage service that allows you to save files online and access them anywhere from any smartphone, tablet, or computer.

Gaming
- **PUBG Mobile or COD Mobile:** Take advantage of the Infinix Note 40 Pro 5G's gaming capabilities with popular mobile games that offer immersive experiences.

Customization
- **Nova Launcher:** Offers advanced features to customize your home screen.
- **Zedge:** Provides a vast selection of free wallpapers, ringtones, app icons, and notification sounds to customize your device easily.

These apps and utilities can help Infinix Note 40 Pro 5G users maximize the capabilities of their devices, whether it's for productivity, photography, entertainment, fitness, or customization.

Community and Online Resources

For Infinix Note 40 Pro 5G users, community and online resources can be invaluable for obtaining support, advice, and the latest information about their devices. Here's how to make the most of these resources.

Official Infinix Support

- **Infinix Support Page:** Visit the official Infinix support page at (**https://wap.infinixmobility.com/care/support**) to learn about Infinix products, view online manuals, get the latest downloads, and more. This page also allows you to connect with other Infinix users and get service, support, and professional advice from Infinix.

Community Forums

- **Infinix Official Community:** Engage with the Infinix community through official forums and social media platforms. These can be valuable resources for troubleshooting and tips and advice from other Infinix users.

Online Manuals and Downloads

- **Access Online Manuals:** The Infinix support page provides online manuals that can help you understand the features and functionalities of your device. These manuals are a great resource for new and experienced users.

- **Download Latest Software:** Keep your device updated by downloading the latest software updates from the Infinix support page. Regular updates can improve performance, add new features, and enhance security.

Professional Advice

- **Get Expert Help:** If you need professional advice, the Infinix support page offers a way to contact Infinix experts who can provide guidance and support for your device-related queries.

Staying Informed
- **Latest News and Updates:** Stay informed about the latest Infinix news, product releases, and updates by regularly visiting the Infinix support page and following Infinix on social media.

By utilizing these community and online resources, Infinix Note 40 Pro 5G users can enhance their understanding of their device, resolve issues, and make the most of their smartphone experience. These resources provide a platform for learning, sharing, and staying connected with the wider Infinix community.

Staying Updated with Infinix News and Releases

For enthusiasts and users of Infinix devices, staying updated with the latest news and releases is important to make the most of their devices. Here are some ways to stay informed about Infinix news and product releases:

Official Infinix Websites
- **Global and Regional Websites:** Visit Infinix's official global website at

(**https://www.infinixmobility.com**) and the regional website for the Philippines at (**https://wap.ph.infinixmobility.com**) to stay updated on the latest product information, news, and updates. These websites often feature the latest devices, announcements, and information about upcoming launches.

Press Releases

- **PR Newswire:** Keep an eye on press releases from Infinix on platforms like PR Newswire, where the company announces new product launches and significant updates. For example, a press release on PR Newswire detailed the launch of the NOTE 40 Series and its innovative features.

Social Media and News Outlets

- **Social Media:** Follow Infinix on social media platforms like Facebook, Twitter, and Instagram for real-time updates, interactive content, and announcements about new products and events.
- **Tech News Websites:** Stay informed by following tech news websites and online

publications like Gadgets 360 and The Business Standard, which cover the latest tech news, including Infinix's product launches and updates.

Community Forums
- **Infinix Official Community:** Engage with the Infinix community through official forums and social media platforms. These can be valuable resources for troubleshooting, tips, and advice from other Infinix users, as well as news about software updates and new product features.

Online Retailers and E-commerce Platforms
- **E-commerce Listings:** Online retailers and e-commerce platforms often list upcoming Infinix mobile phones with expected prices and launch dates. Websites like 91mobiles.com provide a list of upcoming Infinix mobile phones in India, which can be a good source of information for new releases.

By utilizing these resources, Infinix users can stay up-to-date with the latest developments, ensuring they have the most current information about software updates, new product features, and upcoming device launches. This knowledge can help users make informed decisions about purchases, upgrades, and how to get the best out of their Infinix devices.

Appendix

Infinix Note 40 Pro 5G Specifications

- **Brand:** Infinix

- **Model:** Note 40 Pro 5G

- **Launch Date:** Expected to be launched on April 12, 2024

- **Operating System:** Android v14 with XOS 14

- **Display:**
    - 6.78 inches Flexible AMOLED
    - Resolution: 1080 x 2436 pixels (FHD+)
    - Refresh Rate: 120 Hz
    - Pixel Density: 393 ppi
    - Screen Protection: Corning Gorilla Glass
    - Brightness: 1300 nits
    - PWM Dimming: 2160Hz

- Screen to Body Ratio (calculated): 89.33%
- Features: Punch-hole display, Capacitive Touchscreen, Multi-touch

- **Processor:**
    - Chipset: MediaTek Dimensity 7020
    - CPU: Octa-core (2.2 GHz, Dual core, Cortex A78 + 2 GHz, Hexa Core, Cortex A55)
    - Architecture: 64 bit
    - Fabrication: 6 nm
    - Graphics: IMG BXM-8-256

- **Memory:**
    - RAM: 8 GB (LPDDR4X) + Up to 8 GB Extra Virtual RAM
    - Internal Storage: 256 GB (UFS 2.2)
    - Expandable Storage: Yes, up to 1 TB via microSD card

- **Camera:**
    - Rear Camera: Triple - 108 MP (Wide Angle) + 2 MP (Depth Sensor) + 2 MP (Macro) with autofocus
    - Front Camera: 32 MP

- Video Recording: Rear camera - 2K @ 30 fps QHD, 1080p @ 60 fps FHD
- Features: Film, Video, Ai Cam, Portrait, Super Night, Ar Shot, Short Video, Pro, Slow Motion, Dual Video, Panorama, Super Macro
- Flash: Yes, Quad LED

- **Battery:**
    - Capacity: 5000 mAh
    - Type: Li-Po
    - Fast Charging: 45W

- **Connectivity:**
    - SIM: Dual SIM (Nano-SIM, dual stand-by)
    - Network: 5G, 4G, 3G, 2G
    - Wi-Fi: Yes, with Wi-Fi hotspot
    - Bluetooth: Yes, v5.3, A2DP, LE
    - GPS: Yes, with A-GPS
    - USB: USB Type-C 2.0, USB On-The-Go

- **Sensors:**
    - In-Display Fingerprint Sensor
    - Face Unlock
    - Accelerometer, Gyro, Proximity, Compass

- **Additional Features:**
    - Dual Speakers with Sound by JBL
    - IP53 Dust and Splash Resistant
    - NFC
    - 3.5mm Headphone Jack

- **Dimensions:**
    - Width: 75.5 mm
    - Height: 164.28 mm
    - Thickness: 8.09 mm
    - Weight: 196 g

- **Colors:** Vintage Green, Titan Gold

Glossary of Terms

These glossaries cover various topics, from basic mobile phone functionalities to advanced mobile networks and security terminology. Here's a summary of the key areas covered across the sources:

Mobile Technology and Features
- **Smartphone:** A mobile phone with advanced features, including internet connectivity, apps, and often a touchscreen interface.

- **IMEI (International Mobile Equipment Identity):** A unique 15-digit serial number used to identify individual mobile devices.
- **SMS (Short Message Service):** A text messaging service that allows messages to be sent between mobile devices.
- **MMS (Multimedia Messaging Service):** A standard way to send messages that include multimedia content between mobile devices.
- **NFC (Near Field Communication):** A set of communication protocols that enable two electronic devices to establish communication by bringing them within a few centimeters of each other.
- **Bluetooth:** A wireless technology standard for exchanging data over short distances from fixed and mobile devices.
- **Wi-Fi:** A technology for wireless local area networking with devices based on the IEEE 802.11 standards.
- **4G/5G:** Standards for mobile telecommunications that offer faster data transfer rates compared to previous generations (3G).

Mobile Security
- **Encryption:** The process of converting information or data into a code, especially to prevent unauthorized access.
- **Malware:** Malicious software designed to harm or exploit any programmable device, service, or network.
- **Phishing:** A cybercrime in which a target or targets are contacted by email, telephone, or text message by someone posing as a legitimate institution to lure individuals into providing sensitive data.

Mobile Networks & Connectivity
- **GPRS (General Packet Radio Service):** A packet-oriented mobile data standard on the 2G and 3G cellular communication network's global system for mobile communications.
- **GSM (Global Systems for Mobile Communications):** A standard developed to describe protocols for mobile phones' second-generation (2G) digital cellular networks.
- **IP Address (Internet Protocol Address):** A numerical label assigned to

each device connected to a computer network that uses the Internet Protocol for communication.
- **SAR (Specific Absorption Rate):** A measure of the rate at which energy is absorbed by the human body when exposed to a radio frequency electromagnetic field.

User Interface and App Development
- **UI (User Interface):** The means by which the user and a computer system interact, particularly the use of input devices and software.
- **Haptics:** Technology that simulates the sense of touch by applying forces, vibrations, or motions to the user.
- **API (Application Programming Interface):** A set of functions and procedures allowing the creation of applications that access the features or data of an operating system, application, or other service.

These glossaries provide valuable information for understanding the complex terminology associated with mobile devices, networks, security, and application development.

Frequently Asked Questions (FAQs) for Infinix Note 40 Pro 5G

- **Q:** What is the expected Infinix Note 40 Pro 5G launch date in India?
    - **A:** The Infinix Note 40 Pro 5G is scheduled to launch in India on April 12, 2024.
- **Q:** What are the key features of the Infinix Note 40 Pro 5G?
    - **A:** The key features of the Infinix Note 40 Pro 5G include a 6.78-inch full-HD curved AMOLED display with a 120Hz refresh rate, a 108-megapixel main sensor with a triple rear camera setup, MediaTek Dimensity 7020 SoC for seamless multitasking and gaming, and a 5,000mAh battery with 45W fast charging.
- **Q:** Does the Infinix Note 40 Pro 5G support 5G connectivity?

- **A:** Yes, the Infinix Note 40 Pro 5G supports 5G connectivity.

- **Q:** What is the Infinix Note 40 Pro 5G battery capacity, and what charging technologies does it support?
  - **A:** The Infinix Note 40 Pro 5G has a 5,000mAh battery and supports 45W wired fast charging. The Pro+ variant has a 4,600mAh battery and supports 100W charging.

- **Q:** What is the All-Round FastCharge 2.0 technology on the Infinix Note 40 series?
  - **A:** The All-Round FastCharge 2.0 technology on the Infinix Note 40 series includes up to 100W wired charging, wireless charging, reverse wireless charging, magnetic wireless charging, bypass charging, and charging in extreme weather conditions. It also features a magnetic wireless charging power bank and the Cheetah X1 chip for power management.

- **Q:** Can the Infinix Note 40 Pro 5G charge in extreme weather conditions?
  - **A:** Yes, the high-density batteries inside the Note 40 series can withstand extreme cold conditions, even charging the device at minus 20°C.
- **Q:** What audio features does the Infinix Note 40 Pro 5G offer?
  - **A:** The Infinix Note 40 Pro 5G has excellent overall sound quality with good bass, balanced timbre, clarity, localized sound stage, voice expression, and rich detail at high frequencies. It can be branded with JBL.
- **Q:** Where can I find the Infinix Note 40 Pro 5G user manuals and warranty information?
  - **A:** User manuals, warranty information, and FAQs can be found on the official Infinix website at (**https://wap.infinixmobility.com/care/faq**).
- **Q:** How can I access customer support for the Infinix Note 40 Pro 5G?

- **A:** Customer support can be accessed through the official Infinix website, where you can find information on service networks, FAQs, and ways to solve issues.

- **Q:** What are the dimensions and weight of the Infinix Note 40 Pro 5G?
    - **A:** The dimensions of the Infinix Note 40 Pro 5G are not specified in the sources. However, the weight is mentioned as 196 grams.

Legal and Safety Information

General legal and safety information for smartphones, including Infinix devices, typically covers several key areas:

Legal Information

1. **Warranty:** The Infinix Note 40 Pro 5G warranty terms, including the duration and what is covered, are crucial for users to understand their rights and the manufacturer's obligations regarding repairs and replacements.
2. **Intellectual Property:** This includes information about the copyrights,

trademarks, and patents associated with the device's software and hardware. Users are often reminded that certain content and software components are licensed and cannot be copied or distributed without permission.

3. **Regulatory Compliance:** Smartphones must comply with local and international wireless communication, safety, and environmental impact regulations. This includes adherence to standards set by bodies like the FCC (Federal Communications Commission) and CE (Conformité Européenne) in Europe.
4. **Privacy Policy:** Details on how the manufacturer collects, uses, and protects user data. This is particularly relevant for smartphones, as they handle significant personal information.

Safety Information
1. **Battery Use and Charging:** Guidelines on safely charging the device, including using the correct charger and avoiding exposure to extreme temperatures to prevent overheating and potential hazards.

2. **Device Handling:** Instructions on handling the device to avoid damage or injury, such as not attempting to disassemble the device and avoiding contact with liquids.
3. **RF Exposure:** Information on the device's RF (Radio Frequency) energy levels in compliance with regulatory limits and recommendations for minimizing exposure, such as using hands-free options or carrying the device away from the body.
4. **Emergency Calls:** Instructions on making emergency calls, including information on how the device may use location data to assist emergency services.

For specific legal and safety information regarding the Infinix Note 40 Pro 5G, users should refer to the documentation provided with the device or contact Infinix customer support directly. The official Infinix website and support pages may also offer downloadable versions of the user manual and safety guides.

About the Author

William C. Wills is a renowned technology expert and author passionate about demystifying complex devices and empowering users to unlock their full potential. With a career spanning over two decades in the tech industry, he has established himself as a trusted voice in consumer electronics and smart home automation.

Born in Silicon Valley, the epicenter of technological innovation, William was exposed to the ever-evolving world of gadgets and gizmos from a young age. This early exposure ignited a lifelong fascination with technology and a desire to make it accessible to everyone, regardless of their technical expertise.

After graduating from Stanford University with a degree in Computer Science, William embarked on a journey that took him to the forefront of the tech industry. He worked with leading companies, contributing to developing cutting-edge products and services that revolutionized how we live and interact with technology.

www.ingramcontent.com/pod-product-compliance
Lightning Source LLC
Chambersburg PA
CBHW071054240526
45471CB00015B/1898